The Digital Paradigm Shift for a New Business DNA

Andrea Sestino · Luigi Nasta

The Digital Paradigm Shift for a New Business DNA

Implications for Business, Consumers, and Societies

Andrea Sestino
Department of Economics
& Management
Catholic University of Sacred Heart
Rome, Italy

Luigi Nasta
LUISS Guido Carli University
Rome, Italy

ISBN 978-3-031-76237-6   ISBN 978-3-031-76238-3   (eBook)
https://doi.org/10.1007/978-3-031-76238-3

Cover credit: © Harvey Loake

This Palgrave Macmillan imprint is published by the registered company Springer Nature Switzerland AG
The registered company address is: Gewerbestrasse 11, 6330 Cham, Switzerland

If disposing of this product, please recycle the paper.

FOREWORD

A FOREWORD FROM DIGITAL INNOVATION AND MARKETING PERSPECTIVES

It is with great pleasure that I introduce "The Digital Shift Paradigm: New Technologies and Business DNA Empowering Individuals & Societal Wellbeing" authored by Andrea Sestino and Luigi Nasta. This pioneering work explores the transformative potential of digital technologies and their profound impact on individual and societal wellbeing.

As Professor of Digital Marketing and Innovation, I have witnessed firsthand the evolving landscape of digital transformation and its implications across various domains. This book offers a timely and comprehensive exploration of these themes, providing valuable insights for academics, practitioners, and policymakers alike. Moreover, this book is a timely and crucial addition to the body of knowledge in these areas, offering insightful perspectives and practical implications that resonate deeply with my own research, and professional experiences.

In an era where digital transformation is redefining the contours of our personal and professional lives, Sestino and Nasta have adeptly captured the essence of this evolution, extremely important when considering consumers-oriented business strategies.

They highlight how digital technologies are not merely tools for efficiency but are powerful catalysts for enhancing individual satisfaction and societal harmony. The book's emphasis on integrating new technologies into business practices to generate value for both individuals and society is particularly compelling. It aligns perfectly with the emerging paradigm of sustainable business practices that prioritize long-term wellbeing over short-term gains.

From a marketing perspective, the book's holistic approach to understanding the evolving consumer landscape. It goes beyond traditional marketing strategies to explore how digital advancements can foster deeper connections between businesses and consumers. This perspective is critical for marketers seeking to navigate the complexities of the digital age and to create meaningful and sustainable consumer relationships.

The authors also explore the multifaceted relationship between individual wellbeing and digital technology adoption. Their systematic review and empirical studies provide robust evidence on how technologies such as IoT, AI, and mobile health applications can positively influence consumer behaviours and perceptions. This kind of understanding is invaluable for developing marketing strategies that not only meet consumer needs but also enhance their overall quality of life. Furthermore, the exploration of AI-driven tools in the music industry, augmented reality in cultural heritage, and sustainable digital business models in healthcare exemplifies the diverse applications of digital technologies. These case studies underscore the transformative potential of digital innovations across various sectors, offering practical insights that can guide practitioners in designing and implementing technology-driven solutions that are both effective and user-friendly.

Importantly, the book also makes a significant contribution to the discourse on ethical technology deployment.: By emphasizing the need for technologies that promote individual and societal wellbeing, the authors advocate for a balanced approach to innovation—one that considers both economic and humanistic outcomes. This perspective is particularly relevant in today's context, where the ethical implications of technology are under increasing scrutiny.

In conclusion, Sestino and Nasta have provided a comprehensive and thought-provoking exploration of how digital technologies can be harnessed for sustainable progress and social harmony. This volume is a must-read for academics, practitioners, and policymakers who are invested in the future of digital transformation, also because of the useful "Case Studies", and "Specialists' Perspectives" included. It offers a wealth of knowledge and practical guidance that can inspire and inform efforts to leverage digital technologies for the greater good.

Curious about understanding how technologies can contribute to our wellbeing? Fascinated by new technologies and how they can reshape our consumer experiences and positively impact businesses and society?

This book is for you. Enjoy the read.

Professor Yogesh K. Dwivedi
Professor of *Digital Marketing and Innovation*
Founding Director of the *Emerging Markets Research Centre*
(EMaRC)
Co-Director of *Research at the School of Management*, Swansea
University, Wales, UK
Editor-in-Chief, *International Journal of Information Management*

A Foreword from Management and Strategy Perspectives

In an age where the digital landscape is rapidly reshaping every facet of our lives, it is imperative to understand how these technological advancements are influencing strategic decisions and business models. "The Digital Renaissance: New Technologies Empowering Wellbeing for Sustainable Progress and Social Harmony. Implications for Business, Consumers, and Societies", authored by Andrea Sestino and Luigi Nasta, provides an in-depth exploration of this very phenomenon.

As Professor of Corporate Strategy, I have always been intrigued by the intersection of innovation, digital transformation, and strategic business decisions. This book is a significant contribution to the ongoing discourse in this field, offering rich insights and practical implications that will benefit scholars, practitioners, and policymakers alike.

Sestino and Nasta have navigated the complex terrain of digital transformation, shedding light on how new technologies are revolutionizing business models and strategic frameworks. Their work underscores the profound impact of digital innovation on corporate strategy, emphasizing how companies can harness these advancements to drive sustainable growth and competitive advantage. In an environment where traditional business paradigms are constantly being challenged, this book provides a roadmap for navigating the digital frontier.

Beyond the confines of business strategy, "The Digital Renaissance" explores the broader societal implications of digital transformation. The authors examine how digital technologies can contribute to societal well-being, sustainable progress, and social harmony. By highlighting the potential for technology to drive positive social change, they present a holistic view that encompasses both economic and humanistic outcomes. This perspective is especially relevant in today's context, where the ethical and societal implications of technology are under increasing scrutiny.

The book's emphasis on integrating new technologies into business practices to generate value for both individuals and society is particularly compelling. Sestino and Nasta highlight how digital innovations can enhance individual satisfaction and contribute to societal harmony, aligning with the emerging paradigm of sustainable business practices that prioritize long-term wellbeing over short-term gains. Their exploration of AI-driven tools in various sectors, from healthcare to cultural heritage, exemplifies the diverse applications of digital technologies and their potential to foster sustainable progress.

One of the core themes of the book is the role of digital technologies in fostering business model innovation. The authors illustrate how emerging technologies such as artificial intelligence, the Internet of Things, and blockchain are enabling businesses to rethink their value propositions, streamline operations, and enhance customer engagement. These technologies are not just tools for operational efficiency; they are catalysts for creating new business models that are more agile, customer-centric, and sustainable. This perspective is particularly relevant for executives and managers seeking to innovate and stay ahead in a rapidly evolving marketplace.

In conclusion, this book may offer practitioners and scholars a comprehensive framework to navigate the evolving landscape of digital transformation. Indeed, by exploring its implications for business, consumers, and societies, this insightful book illuminates strategic pathways towards fostering sustainable progress and social harmony. The authors have provided a valuable resource that will inspire and inform efforts to leverage digital innovation for strategic advantage, societal wellbeing, and sustainable progress. This book is an essential reading for anyone interested in understanding the profound impact of digital transformation on business and society. It offers a wealth of knowledge and practical guidance that will undoubtedly shape the future of strategic decision-making in the digital age.

Professor Paolo Boccardelli
Rector, *Luiss University*, Rome, Italy
Professor of *Corporate Strategy*
Founding Director of the research center *Strategic Change "Franco Fontana"*, Rome, Italy

ACKNOWLEDGEMENTS

The authors would like to express our deepest gratitude to each other for the unwavering support and collaboration that made this book possible.

Our heartfelt thanks also go to *everyone* who offered personal support, emotional encouragement, and warmth throughout this journey.

Additionally, we are profoundly grateful to all the professionals whose expertise and contributions were invaluable in the creation of this volume: Your dedication and assistance have been instrumental in bringing our vision to life.

Firstly, the authors would like to thank Prof. *Yogesh K. Dwivedi* (Professor of Digital Marketing & Innovation, School of Management, Swansea University, United Kingdom), and Prof. *Paolo Boccardelli* (Rector, and Professor of Management & Strategy, LUISS Guido Carli University, Rome), who contributed to the creation of the Foreword, each with a rigorous analysis of the topics addressed in the volume from their evaluable own perspective.

Importantly, the authors would also like to thank the researchers, professionals, managers, scholars, and practitioners who contributed to this book with their "Case Insights Box", shedding light on important case studies related to companies engaged in the issues of exploiting new technologies in their value propositions potentially positively affecting individuals' and societies' wellbeing, and their "Specialists' Perspectives" related to in-depth analyses and perspectives of experts and professionals presented in the book.

Specifically, as for the "Case Insights Box", the authors would like to thank: *Piergiovanni Mazzoli*, Scientific Director, VR-For-Care; *Matteo Marciano*, Associate Professor of Music Technology New York University, Mixer, Sound Designer; *Valeria Morè*, Communication Manager, Agricolus s.r.l.; *Camilla Larini*, CTO DigitalRehab; *Silvia Sciamanna*, COO DigitalRehab; *Giuseppe Recchia*, CEO DigitalRehab; *Eugenio Luciani*, Business Advisor DigitalRehab; *Martina Marchese*, Project Manager, Travel Verse; *Mariagrazia Efato*, President of Association surfHers, Co-founder Tawave. As for the "Specialists' Perspectives" we would finally like to thank, *Alfredo Sagona*, International Business Development Consultant, and *Cristina Dachille*, Strategy & Sustainability Manager, CDP Venture Capital SGR, Rome, Italy.

CONTENTS

ABOUT THE AUTHORS

Andrea Sestino (Ph.D., Qualified as Associate Professor in *Management & Marketing Studies*) is Research Fellow and Adjunct Professor of Management & Marketing Studies at the Catholic University of Sacred Heart, specifically involved in new technologies, innovation and management studies and its impact on both business and consumers. Moreover, he is also Adjunct Professor of "Fundamentals of Management", and "Competitive Strategy" at the LUISS Guido Carli University, and of "Marketing" and "Strategy" at the LUISS Business School, in Rome. He has been Visiting Lecturer and Researcher at the School of Business, Innovation and Sustainability, Halmstad University, in Sweden.

Andrea holds a Ph.D. in the Management & Marketing field at the Ionian Department of Law, Economics, Environment, University of Bari Aldo Moro, and an M.Sc. in Management at Sapienza University, Rome, Italy. He has been also Research Fellow at the University of Rome Tre, *Expert Collaborator* for the Cabinet of the Italian Minister of Economic Development, and *Expert* for the *EU Commission*, in fields related to Artificial Intelligence, Internet of Things applications, and business digitalization, and *R&D Specialist* particularly concerning the digital transformation of enterprises and the processes of technological evolution, for both private and public research projects.

He has published a book, and several articles in international peer-reviewed journals, such as *Technovation, Technological Forecasting and Social Change, Technology Analysis & Strategic Management, European*

Journal of Innovation Management, Management Decision, Technology in Society, Journal of Retailing and Consumer Services, Journal of Small Business & Enterprise Development, Global Business Review, International Journal of Healthcare and Pharmaceutical Marketing, SN Business & Economics, and so on.

He is also part of the Editorial Board of the *European Journal of Innovation Management, British Food Journal, Economics, Management & Financial Market,* and *International Journal of Electronic Trade.*

Luigi Nasta (Ph.D.) is Assistant Professor of Management at John Cabot University (Rome, Italy), where he teaches courses including "Principles of Management", "Entrepreneurship in Creative Industries", "Early-Stage Entrepreneurship", and "Strategic Consulting". Additionally, he serves as Research Fellow and Adjunct Professor of Management at Luiss Business School (Rome, Italy), with a focus on research activities within the Creative Industry Competence Center. He also holds the position of Adjunct Professor of "Creative Industries and Business Model Innovation" at Luiss University (Rome, Italy).

Prof. Nasta earned a Ph.D. in Management from the Department of Business and Management at Luiss University in Rome, Italy, where he also completed his M.Sc. in Management.

He was a visiting researcher in the ARC Centre of Excellence for Creative Industries and Innovation (CCI) at Queensland University of Technology. His research work in the field of digitalization, business model, technology acceptance, and sustainability was published in peer-reviewed journals including *Finance Research Letters, Journal of Business Models, Journal of General Management, Sustainability, International Journal of Business Research and Management (IJBRM), Creative Industries Journal, Journal of International Accounting Research, Management Decision, Corporate Social Responsibility and Environmental Management, Technology in Society, European Journal of Cultural Management and Policy, International Journal of Auditing Technology,* and chapters for Springer, Routledge, and IntechOpen books.

LIST OF FIGURES

LIST OF TABLES

Introduction. Evolving Consumers, Firms, and Societies. Do We Remember Why Companies *Exist*?

Abstract This chapter examines recent societal changes and their impact on consumers, companies, and societies from a holistic perspective. It revisits the fundamental purpose of companies, contrasting their profit-driven nature with their original goal of meeting individual needs. Emphasizing a consumer-oriented approach, it argues for integrating marketing activities coherently across various perspectives. The chapter stresses the importance of focusing on value generation and profit margins rather than just sales volumes. By reasserting the true purpose of companies, it introduces key themes: the book's rationale goes beyond traditional views, highlighting how new technologies, when effectively integrated into business activities, can create value for individuals and society. This fosters a sustainable business orientation that enhances overall wellbeing and maximizes individual satisfaction. The discussion illustrates how businesses can align with a sustainable agenda, benefiting both consumers and society through the strategic use of digital advancements.

Keywords Technologies · Digital technologies · Consumers · Companies · Societies · Needs · Humanity · Wellbeing · Sustainable orientation · Needs satisfaction

© The Author(s), under exclusive license to Springer Nature Switzerland AG 2025
A. Sestino and L. Nasta, *The Digital Paradigm Shift for a New Business DNA*, https://doi.org/10.1007/978-3-031-76238-3_1

1

1.1   Introduction. How Have *New* *Technologies* Changed Our Lives?

The advent of digital transformation and the emergence of new technologies have profoundly impacted both businesses and society, bringing about a radical transformation (Kraus et al., 2021; Sestino et al., 2023; Strømmen-Bakhtiar, 2020; Van Veldhoven & Vanthienen, 2022). The integration of new technologies (e.g., as for the *Internet of Things*, the *Artificial Intelligence*, the *Blockchain*, the *Virtual* and *Augmented Reality*, and so on) has revolutionized traditional business models, enhancing efficiency, connectivity, and accessibility.

This shift has not only redefined the way companies operate but has also significantly influenced societal norms and interactions (Dąbrowska et al., 2022). From streamlined processes to unprecedented connectivity, the digital age has ushered in a new era of possibilities, fundamentally altering the landscape of how individuals live and work.

In recent years, the focal point of research and practical efforts within the realms of business, management, and marketing, practice has been directed towards the optimization and maximization of the benefits derived from emerging technologies.

This strategic orientation is rooted in the recognition of the transformative potential inherent in these technologies, prompting a concerted effort to integrate them comprehensively into various facets of organizational operations. The philosophy of "technologies in service of humanity", as eloquently proposed by Kotler (2022), has garnered widespread consensus, encapsulating the ethos that these advancements should not only enhance operational efficiency and profitability but also contribute positively to societal wellbeing. This guiding principle underscores a holistic approach wherein technological innovations are harnessed not merely for commercial gains but with a conscientious consideration of their broader implications on human welfare and societal advancement.

In this technology-infused landscape, also characterized by the profound heterogeneity among the final end users (e.g., as for the consumers), the approaches of marketing and management have undergone significant transformations.

If traditionally the management and marketing approaches referred to the broader field encompassing activities related to promoting and selling products or services, with a focus on understanding consumers' needs and creating value, on the other hand, today the "new" marketing management specifically denotes also the organizational and strategic aspects of overseeing and implementing marketing activities within a company. While marketing involves the entire process of identifying consumer needs, designing products, determining pricing strategies, and promoting offerings, marketing management pertains to the planning, coordination, and control of these activities within the context of overall business objectives.

Notably, certain researchers have coined the expression "marketing: the management oriented to the market" intending not only the imperative for all business activities to be aligned with market dynamics and for management to functionally respond to such imperatives, but also the acknowledgement of the centrality of marketing approaches (Harris, 2022; Webster Jr., 2005). Such an approach particularly underscores the significance of prioritizing the consumers in business choices and emphasizes the need for management practices to actively engage in and resonate with marketing principles.

In this domain, in incorporating new technologies, companies not only have to integrate such advancements within production processes, but particularly within the final value propositions enriched by innovative technological features. In the present landscape, companies are challenged to conscientiously consider not only the pronounced heterogeneity among the final beneficiaries of these efforts, i.e., the consumers, but also to actively strive towards enabling them to derive maximum benefit from the introduction of such technologies. This strategic imperative extends beyond mere operational considerations, emphasizing a concerted effort to enhance consumer satisfaction and contribute to the amelioration of their overall wellbeing.

1.2   Evolving Consumers

1.2.1   Four Pillars of Management and Marketing Studies

As delineated by the seminal literature in the fields of management and marketing studies, four fundamental principles govern the actions of businesses: (1) all consumers are different; (2) all consumers change; (3) all competitor reacts; (4) resources are scarce by nature (Fig. 1.1).

By profoundly analysing such pillars, firstly, the recognition that all consumers exhibit inherent diversity and heterogeneity underscores the

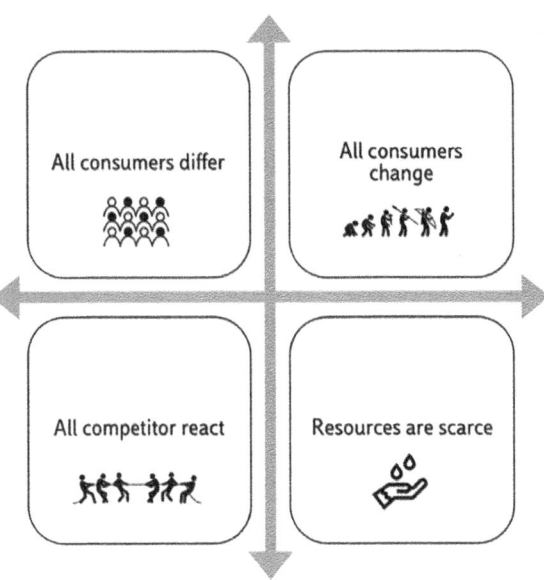

Fig. 1.1 Four principles (*Source* Authors' elaboration, adapted from Palmatier & Crecelius, 2019)

imperative for companies to comprehend and navigate the varied needs and preferences of their "clientele". Secondly, the acknowledgement that disparities among consumers persist emphasizes the dynamic and evolving nature of consumer behaviour, necessitating a precise and adaptable approach.

Moreover, the principle that all competitors react underscores the competitive dynamics inherent in the business environment, highlighting the need for strategic foresight and responsiveness to maintain a competitive edge. Lastly, the acknowledgement of the scarcity of resources underscores the necessity for judicious resource allocation and management, necessitating prudent decision-making to optimize operational efficiency and effectiveness (Fig. 1.2).

Not coincidentally, over the past decades, there has been a discernible shift in focus within business paradigms, particularly regarding the attention to final consumers.

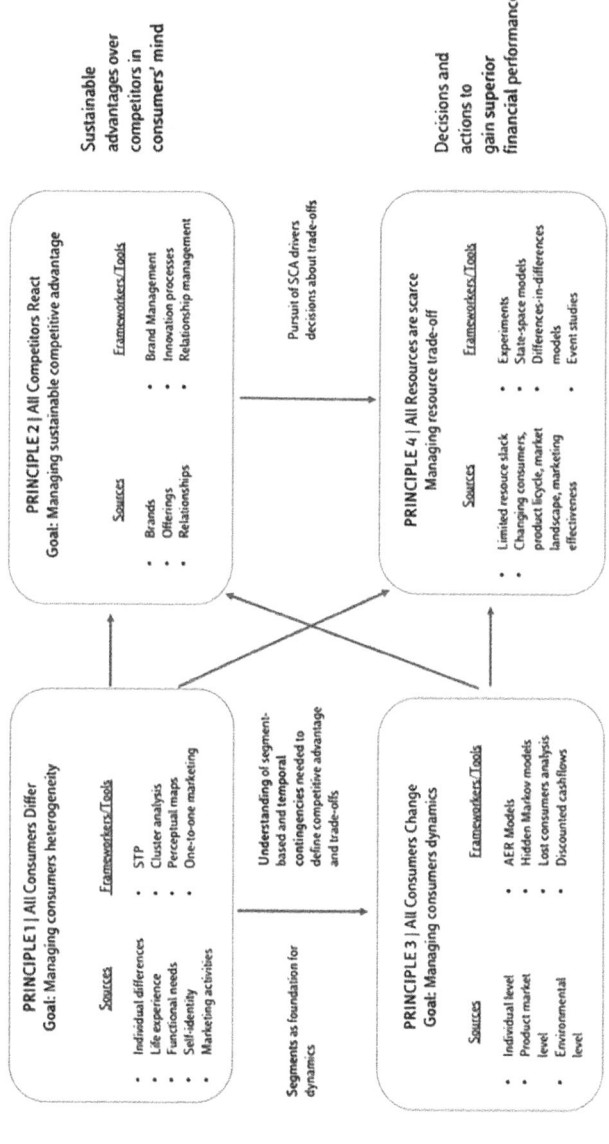

Fig. 1.2 Integrating the four principles (*Source* Authors' elaboration of Palmatier & Crecelius, 2019)

This evolution may be attributed to the dynamic socio-economic landscape, where consumers have become increasingly discerning, empowered, and central to business success. Contemporary businesses are, therefore, compelled to adopt a "consumer-centric" orientation, a strategic approach that places the consumer at the core of decision-making processes.

The "consumer-centric" orientation is characterized by a "philosophy" that prioritizes and revolves around the needs, preferences, and satisfaction of the final consumers. Indeed, such an approach emphasizes a profound understanding of consumers' behaviour, preferences, and expectations, positioning the consumer as the focal point of decision-making processes and strategic initiatives. In this paradigm, the business endeavours to tailor its products, services, and overall value proposition to align seamlessly with consumers' requirements, aiming to enhance consumer experience and build long-term relationships. In this light, as Kotler and Armstrong (2018) suggested, a consumer-centric approach should involve not only recognizing the diversity among consumers but also actively engaging with them to anticipate and fulfil their evolving needs, thereby fostering loyalty and sustaining competitive advantage.

1.2.2   Why Are Individuals Pivotal in the Discourse Surrounding New Technologies?

In the context of integrating new technologies into products or services, the imperative of an "individual-centric" or "consumer-centric" approach becomes even more pronounced. As technological advancements continue to reshape the business landscape, companies are confronted with the challenge of not merely incorporating these innovations within their operational frameworks, but doing so in a manner that resonates with the diverse and evolving needs of the end users. A consumer-centric orientation becomes indispensable in ensuring the efficacy and efficiency of technological integration into the business's value proposition.

By prioritizing the role of the final consumers in the integration of new technologies as a part of innovation business strategies, the organization may thus tailor their offerings to align seamlessly with consumer preferences and expectations. Thus, this approach not only enhances the market relevance of products or services but also contributes significantly to consumer satisfaction. Furthermore, considering the diverse demographics and preferences of consumers, a consumer-centric approach ensures that technological features are not only incorporated for the sake of innovation but are strategically designed to add tangible value to the consumer experience.

Hence, in these technological endeavours, the objective extends beyond mere acknowledgement of the consumer's significance as the recipient of corporate strategies, innovation efforts in products and services, and the like. The overarching aim is to ensure a highly personalized value proposition that resonates effectively with end consumers. Simultaneously, the broader aspiration is to leverage these new technologies not only to enhance the customized nature of offerings but also to contribute, through technological advancements, to the overall wellbeing of the end users. This aligns with the paradigm of "technologies in service of humanity", underscoring a commitment not only to meeting consumer expectations but also to actively elevating their final state of wellbeing through thoughtful technological integration.

1.3 Evolving Companies and Organizations

1.3.1 Business Changes and Digital Transformation

The incorporation of new technologies into the value proposition of businesses is a multifaceted process that spans various aspects of organizational operations. Primarily, companies integrate these technologies along their production processes by leveraging advanced automation, robotics, and data analytics to enhance efficiency and precision. In product design, the integration of technologies is evident through the incorporation of features such as IoT connectivity, artificial intelligence algorithms, and augmented reality interfaces, exemplified by smart home devices or wearable technology.

Moreover, businesses are increasingly integrating technology into the delivery of services, fostering innovation in service provision. For instance, the implementation of AI-powered chatbots for consumer support or mobile apps that leverage location-based services for personalized experiences exemplifies this trend. These innovations not only enhance consumer engagement but also streamline service delivery.

To achieve such integration, companies embark on ongoing digital transformation journeys, necessitating fundamental changes in management approaches, organizational culture, and structures. This transformative process aims to align the entire business ecosystem with digital imperatives. This includes fostering a culture of adaptability, restructuring organizational frameworks to accommodate agile methodologies, and revisiting traditional business models to incorporate digital elements.

For instance, recent studies (i.e., Sestino et al., 2024), by employing and holistic view inspired by a marketing management-oriented approach, underlined how such a perspective is crucial to ensure full comprehension of the multifaceted influences shaping the digital transformation of companies, because affecting internal-related and external-related companies' components. Specifically, the study explained that viewed through the lens of internal marketing management, the digitalization process presents challenges in addressing the resistance to change among internal resources directly involved: It also involves the dissemination of digital culture as a novel philosophy, aiming to render this transition positively perceptible and successful.

Conversely, this transformation necessitates the inclusion of new and highly competent individuals, particularly those capable of spreading the new digital transformation culture, with newer skills (e.g., as for *e-leadership* skills, in "leading" the digitalization-based cultural change; Iacono, 2021), and overall, by considering its impact on new leadership approaches (Acciarini et al., 2024).

Indeed, given the current disruptive environmental changes, such as digitalization, which can potentially disrupt strategies, decision-making processes, and leadership, it is essential to understand the new role of leaders and their capabilities (Boccardelli & Brunetta, 2024). Moreover, from an external marketing management standpoint, digital transformation may result in an opportunity to expedite the evolution of production processes, leading to heightened quality, efficiency, and effectiveness. Simultaneously, it enhances the competitive prowess of a firm within an intensely competitive business landscape (Fig. 1.3).

In some circumstances, businesses adopt or organically evolve into digital business models, where the digital component is not just an augmentation but a foundational aspect of their core business strategies. Overall, this transformative landscape underscores the imperative for businesses to continually evolve and embrace digitalization as an intrinsic part of their strategic vision.

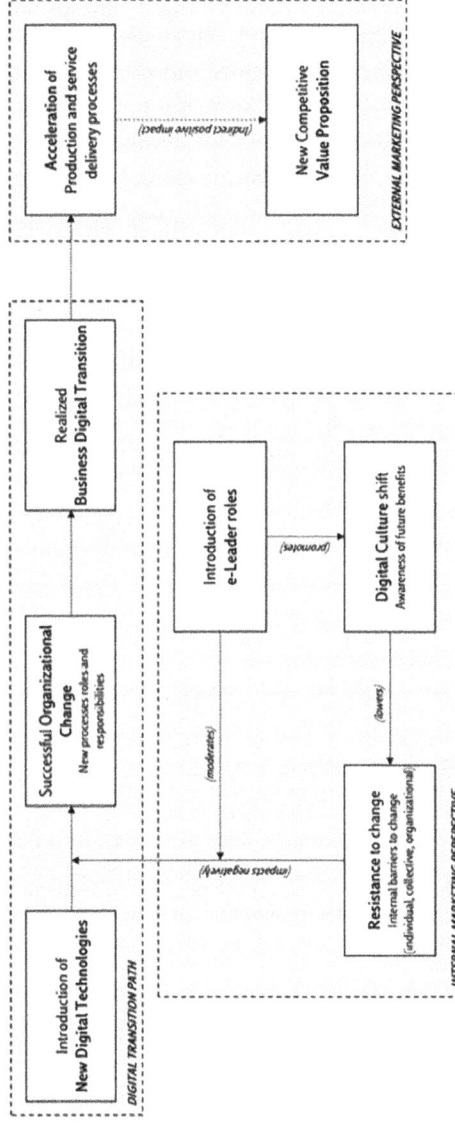

Fig. 1.3 The digital transformation framework: an internal and an external marketing management perspective (*Source* Author's elaboration drawn from Sestino et al., 2024)

1.3.2   Business Model vs. Digital Business Models

All organizations operate within a defined logic, encapsulated by the concept of the so-called "business model", which serves as a fundamental framework delineating the core components and operational dynamics of a business.

A business model encompasses the structural elements that delineate how an organization creates, delivers, and captures value (Osterwalder & Pigneur, 2010). This concept is comprised of key building blocks, including consumer segments, value propositions, channels, consumer relationships, revenue streams, key resources, key activities, key partnerships, and cost structure (Osterwalder & Pigneur, 2010), as shown in the Table 1.1.

The consumer segments elucidate the target audience, while the value propositions articulate the offerings that address consumer needs. Channels and consumer relationships delineate the mechanisms through which products or services are delivered and how consumer interactions are

Table 1.1   Components of a business model

Component	Description
Consumer Segments	Identification of the target audience or groups of consumers the business aims to serve
Value Proposition	Clear articulation of the unique value the business offers to its consumers, addressing their needs or solving their problems
Channels	The various channels or means through which the business delivers its products or services to consumers
Consumer Relationships	Describes the types of relationships the business establishes and maintains with its consumers
Revenue Streams	The avenues through which the business generates income, specifying pricing strategies and revenue sources
Key Resources	The essential assets, capabilities, and infrastructure required to deliver the value proposition and "manage" the business
Key Activities	The core activities and processes the business engages in to create and deliver its value proposition
Key Partnerships	Collaborative relationships with external entities that contribute to the overall success of the business
Cost Structure	Breakdown of the costs associated with operating the business, including fixed and variable costs

Source Author's elaboration

managed. Revenue streams elucidate the avenues through which the business generates income, while the key resources, activities, and partnerships underscore the essential elements and collaborations required for the model's functionality. Finally, the cost structure delineates the incurred expenses (Osterwalder & Pigneur, 2010).

By considering the current hyper-technological scenario, the distinction between a traditional business model undergoing digital transformation and a native digital business model lies in their fundamental inception and orientation towards digital strategies.

A traditional business model embarking on digital transformation typically represents an existing entity that integrates digital technologies to enhance its operational efficiency, consumer engagement, and overall competitiveness (Porter & Heppelmann, 2014), also shown in the proposed *Digital Transformation Framework* above (Sestino et al., 2024).

Such an adaptation involves integrating digital components into existing processes and structures, often necessitating a cultural shift and adjustments to legacy systems. An illustrative example is the transformation of a brick-and-mortar retail store implementing e-commerce platforms and digital marketing strategies to expand its reach and improve consumer experiences.

Conversely, a "native" digital business model is inherently conceived and built upon digital foundations, exemplifying an organization born within the digital landscape and characterized by an intrinsic alignment with digital technologies from its inception (Amit & Zott, 2015; Zott & Amit, 2010). Such models leverage digital platforms, data analytics, and agile methodologies as core components of their value proposition and operational framework. An iconic illustration is the business model of digital platforms like Airbnb (i.e., the famous digital platform for apartment or b&b booking services) or Uber for taxis, where the entire service delivery, from matchmaking to transactions, is facilitated through digital interfaces, or Doctolib, one of the most important platforms for digital-based healthcare services (e.g., as for medical teleconsultation).

In essence, while both models undergo digitalization processes, the native digital business model is distinguished by its organic inception in the digital realm, affording it a unique and often more seamless integration of digital strategies throughout its structure and operations.

1.4   Do We Remind Why Firms Exist?

1.4.1   A World of Firms, Organizations, Entities

In contemporary society, the proliferation of companies, organizations, corporations, entities, and institutions is so pervasive that individuals often find themselves surrounded by a multitude of these entities without a comprehensive awareness of their collective presence.

To date, there were over 200 million registered businesses globally, encompassing a diverse array of industries and scales (World Bank, 2021). Among the most notable and globally recognized companies are technology giants like Apple, Microsoft, and Amazon, each boasting significant market capitalization and substantial annual revenues: For instance, as of the year 2021, Apple reported a revenue of approximately $365 billion, Microsoft around $168 billion, and Amazon an impressive $386 billion (Statista, 2021). These companies exemplify the scale and economic influence of contemporary corporations, contributing significantly to the global economy.

1.4.2   The Rationale Behind the Existence of Companies

The rationale behind the existence of companies is deeply rooted in multifaceted considerations that converge to fulfil essential economic, social, and strategic imperatives. From an economic standpoint, firms serve as vital engines of production and distribution, driving innovation, generating employment, and contributing to overall economic growth (Fama & Jensen, 1983). Socially, businesses play a pivotal role in fostering community development, providing goods and services that meet diverse needs, and creating a network of interdependencies that sustains societal progress (Matten & Moon, 2008).

Strategically, the existence of companies may be attributed to their adeptness in capitalizing on synergies and efficiencies that arise from organizational structures, facilitating the pooling of resources, expertise, and efforts to achieve common objectives (Barney, 1991; Barney et al., 2021). The imperative for companies to create and capture value within the market ecosystem also propels their existence, with each entity acting as a nexus for value creation that extends beyond mere economic transactions.

The Authors here formally suggest that firms and companies exist for two distinct purposes: (1) an "original" purpose and (2) an "institutional" purpose. Regarding the original purpose, businesses are conceived with the goal of fulfilling needs, addressing scarce resources, and ultimately contributing to societal wellbeing (see the Fig. 1.4).

In this context, companies are established to serve as mechanisms for the satisfaction of human needs, rectification of resource scarcities, and the overall enhancement of social welfare. By considering the institutional purpose, irrespective of their current classification as profit-oriented, nonprofit, or other designations, businesses are inherently mandated to create value. This value creation, often manifested in financial gains, is integral to the overarching goal of sustaining and perpetuating the institution, reflecting the broader institutional imperative of businesses to contribute positively to economic landscapes and stakeholder interests.

Therefore, it is clear that firms, in their "life", are duty-bound to satisfy the needs of end consumers and, more broadly, the society, while concurrently ensuring the preservation of the surrounding environment. This imperative gives rise to the contemporary emphasis on the sustainability of productive activities, where sustainability denotes the fulfilment of the

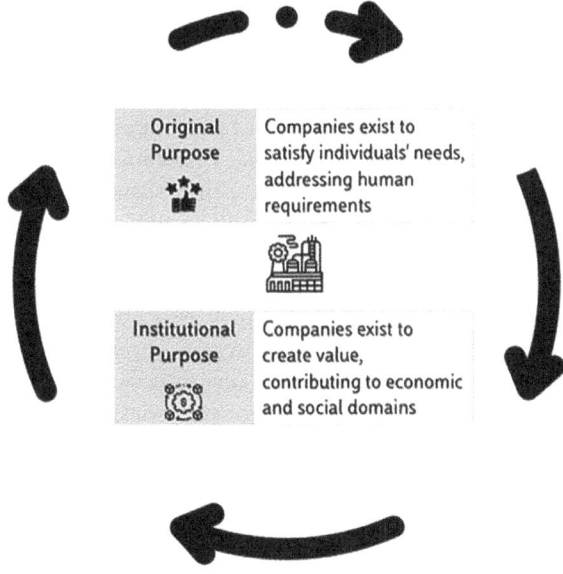

Fig. 1.4 Why companies exist? Original *vs.* Institutional purposes (*Source* Authors' elaboration)

needs of the present community without compromising the wellbeing of[*] future societies.

Sustainability and Business Strategies
Indeed, by focusing on sustainability, such a term in a formal academic context refers to the capacity of systems, processes, or activities to endure and persist over time while concurrently meeting the needs of the present without compromising the ability of future generations to meet their own needs (World Commission on Environment and Development, 1987), importantly, not only from a "mere" environmental perspective.

Such an orientation, indeed, embodies a holistic approach encompassing environmental, social, and economic dimensions, emphasizing the harmonious integration of these facets. As articulated by Elkington (1997), sustainability entails the pursuit of a triple bottom line, wherein businesses strive to optimize not only economic gains but also social equity and environmental stewardship.

Based on the above, this paradigm underscores the crucial balance between meeting current societal needs and safeguarding the prospects of forthcoming generations. The ongoing debates, research endeavours, and industrial efforts surrounding perennial and weighty issues such as pollution exemplify the conscientious drive within businesses to navigate and mitigate the environmental impact of their operations.

Importantly, by considering *Political, Economical, Social, Technological, Environmental,* and *Legal* factors, being sustainable may not only assume an important meaning, but should inspire companies' activities, as described in the Table 1.2.

Specifically, from the *Political* perspective, sustainability necessitates active participation in transparent political processes and advocacy for policies aligning with ethical business practices. *Economically*, sustainable practices involve the implementation of fair-trade policies, ensuring equitable outcomes, and considering the broader social and environmental impacts of business operations. *Social sustainability* is characterized by a commitment to fostering diversity, ensuring fair labour practices, and contributing positively to community development. Moreover, from a *Technological* perspective, sustainability entails the adoption of innovative solutions that align with environmental and social responsibility goals, promoting energy efficiency and minimizing ecological impact. Furthermore, *Environmental* sustainability emphasizes eco-friendly practices, resource conservation, and carbon footprint reduction, requiring

Table 1.2 Sustainable business strategies from a political, economic, social, technological, environmental, and legal perspective

Aspects	Strategies for business sustainability
Political	Engage in transparent political lobbying, support ethical political candidates
Economical	Implement fair-trade practices, promote inclusive economic growth
Social	Foster diversity and inclusion, contribute to community development
Technological	Embrace innovation, invest in sustainable technologies
Environmental	Adopt eco-friendly practices, reduce carbon footprint
Legal	Ensure compliance with environmental regulations, uphold ethical standards

businesses to actively engage in conservation efforts. Finally, in terms of *Legal* perspective, sustainability involves ensuring compliance with environmental regulations and upholding ethical standards in business operations, contributing to a regulatory environment that supports long-term sustainability.

1.5   THE NEED OF A NEW PHILOSOPHY
AND A RENEWED DNA, FOR A DIGITAL SHIFT PARADIGM

1.5.1   A New Holistic Philosophy

Coherently with the principles of sustainability and conscious of the inherent "original" orientation of businesses towards satisfying the needs of the collective, together with the emphasized consumer-centricity approaches, there arises a compelling imperative to cultivate a trajectory focused on the integration of new technologies.

This trajectory should extend beyond the mere fulfilment of needs and necessities, aspiring instead towards the ambitious end goal of collectively enhancing societal wellbeing. Recognizing that technological advancements have the potential not only to meet current demands but also to fundamentally elevate the quality of life for communities at large, businesses are encouraged to adopt a strategic paradigm that transcends immediate satisfaction and actively contributes to the holistic improvement of societal welfare.

This forward-thinking approach, and the "philosophy" behind this reasoning, aligns with the ethos of sustainable development and underscores the transformative power of technology in fostering a more prosperous and equitable future for society as a whole, also, emphasizing the crucial and essential role of management and marketing efforts, especially in the case of new technologies, for improving and enhancing the societies' wellbeing.

1.5.2   Digital Technologies and Innovation to "Remember" Firms' Core Purpose, for a New Business DNA

The emerging paradigm that businesses we propose in the book and that firms should adopt emphasizes the fundamental principle of "remembering" their core purpose, which is to fulfil the needs of consumers and communities. By realigning their strategic focus towards this foundational objective, enterprises can leverage the vast opportunities afforded by digital technologies to redesign their value propositions.

Such an approach not only may enhance consumers' satisfaction but also promote sustainable development and community wellbeing. In essence, by integrating digital innovation with a purpose-driven mission, businesses can achieve a symbiotic relationship between technological advancement and societal benefit, thereby securing their long-term relevance and success. Importantly, in such a context it's imperative to remind the notion of the so-called "firm's DNA", which refers to the unique combination of elements that define its identity, including its culture, values, capabilities, and operational processes, introduced by Chris Zook and James Allen in their book "Profit from the Core: Growth Strategy in an Era of Turbulence" (Zook & Allen, 2001).

Therefore, the awareness of the disruptive potential of new technologies, combined with their effective utilization to propose new value propositions, also impacts culture (i.e., through the spread of a new organizational culture resulting from the introduction of new technologies; e.g., as in Hemerling et al. 2018; Sestino et al., 2020; Wang et al., 2024), values (i.e., by driving company values to be technology-driven; e.g., as in Bounfour, 2016; Wolf, 2017), capabilities (i.e., as upskilling and reskilling become necessary to better embrace digital components within the company, also by promoting a new digital leadership; e.g., as in Boccardelli, 2018; Bresciani et al., 2021a; Demir et al., 2019; Sestino et al., 2024), and operational processes (i.e., in the restructuring of operational processes that lead to value creation or service delivery; e.g., as in Plekhanov et al., 2022; Zaoui & Souissi, 2020). When these elements are oriented not only towards profit but also towards enhancing the wellbeing of individuals and society, they inevitably impact and transform the DNA of firms.

1.6   Organization and Structure of the Book

Thus, by following our reasoning and the new suggested holistic philosophy, this book provides an in-depth exploration of how digital technologies can be leveraged to enhance individual and societal wellbeing. It does so by examining the evolving role of companies, the interaction between technology and consumer behaviour, and the implications for various sectors, particularly healthcare and cultural heritage. The book is structured to first establish a theoretical foundation, then propose four specific empirical studies, and finally synthesize these insights into actionable strategies and policy recommendations.

Chapter 2 provides a comprehensive literature review on the relationship between individual wellbeing and reactions to new digital technologies. Through a systematic review process, the chapter identifies key contributions and synthesizes them to highlight how different technologies impact individual wellbeing across various settings such as healthcare, tourism, music, and cultural heritage. The review lays the groundwork for understanding how emerging digital trends can shape effective management and marketing strategies.

By focusing on mobile health technologies, Chapter 3 investigates their role in transforming healthcare delivery and their impact on patient wellbeing. Through an experimental study with 175 participants, it examines how digital technologies in patient monitoring can enhance positive reactions, such as the intention to use these technologies and engage in positive word-of-mouth. The study highlights the mediating role of perceived wellbeing in these effects, offering insights into the positive use of technology in healthcare.

Conversely, Chapter 4 then explores the emotional impacts of AI-based music recommendation systems. It investigates how perceived ease of use and perceived usefulness of AI tools influence positive emotions and trust among users. Through a survey of 242 individuals and Structural Equation Modelling, the study reveals that these factors significantly enhance emotional responses, which, in turn, foster trust in AI tools. The findings have practical implications for designing emotionally engaging and trustworthy AI systems.

In Chapter 5, we focus on the role of Augmented Reality and Life Satisfaction in Cultural Heritage. Indeed, by examining the role of augmented reality (AR) and gamification in cultural heritage experiences, this chapter investigates how these technologies enhance visitor enjoyment and engagement. Using data from 164 participants, it analyses how the perceived usefulness and ease of use of AR technology contribute to enjoyment, engagement, and ultimately, life satisfaction. The study underscores the importance of designing user-friendly AR applications to maximize their educational and entertainment value.

Lastly, Chapter 6 presents a qualitative case study of Pyllola, an Italian startup offering telemedicine services. It explores how sustainable digital business models (SDBMs) can facilitate access to healthcare, create value, and enhance individual and societal wellbeing. The study highlights the positive impacts of SDBMs on value creation, delivery, and capture, emphasizing the sustainability component as crucial for achieving these outcomes.

Finally, Chapter 7 synthesizes the insights from the previous chapters, integrating the literature review and empirical studies to provide a holistic view of digital technology integration. It discusses theoretical, managerial, marketing, and policy implications, offering guidance for scholars, practitioners, and stakeholders on the ethical and effective use of digital technologies. The chapter emphasizes the role of these technologies in redefining value propositions and enhancing individual and societal wellbeing. Importantly, among the book, some "Case Insights Box" related to firms dealing with the issue of integrating new technologies into their value proposition also in the attempt to contribute to individuals' and societal wellbeing, together with some "Specialist's Perspective" boxes, prepared by managers, scholars, and practitioners are provided.

The book ultimately aims to transcend traditional views on business and technology by focusing on how digital advancements can generate value for individuals and society. By exploring various sectors and integrating theoretical and empirical insights, it provides a comprehensive guide for leveraging digital technologies in a sustainable and consumer-oriented manner.

CHAPTER 2

The Relationship Between Individuals' Wellbeing and Individuals' Reactions to New Digital Technologies: A Review

Abstract The topic of individual wellbeing has frequently been debated in the literature, given its varied definitions and measurement methodologies, as well as the diverse settings in which it has been applied. In this chapter, we conducted a systematic literature review: The selection process involved a careful examination of identified articles for alignment with research objectives and subsequent content analysis through data extrapolation. A total of 112 documents were initially identified, and after successive screening processes, only 52 relevant contributions were selected for in-depth analysis, as they were strictly related to the topic under investigation. These contributions were further synthesized, aligning with the consumer behaviour perspective, to stimulate discussions on designing effective management and marketing strategies based on emerging topics and future trends dealing with the effect of new technological integrations on individuals' wellbeing, by considering the technology investigated in such contributions. The results shed light on the combined effects of the most widespread wellbeing measurement methodologies in relation to the integration of new technologies (IoT, Big Data, VR and AR, AI, and so on) and their impact on individuals, as well as the most relevant research settings and industries worthy of attention and future investigation.

© The Author(s), under exclusive license to Springer Nature Switzerland AG 2025
A. Sestino and L. Nasta, *The Digital Paradigm Shift for a New Business DNA*, https://doi.org/10.1007/978-3-031-76238-3_2

Keywords Technologies · Digital technologies · Wellbeing · PERMA model · Healthcare · Tourism · Music · Cultural heritage · Emotions · Engagement · Relationship · Accomplishment · Security · Sustainable development

2.1   Introduction

The integration of new technologies, encompassing the Internet of Things (IoT), smart objects, artificial intelligence (AI), blockchain, and chatbots, has become a central focus across management, technology, and marketing disciplines (Hoffman et al., 2022).

Such new technologies infusions into contemporary society, and specifically into product features in contributing to deliver renewed services, bear substantial implications for the wellbeing of end users. The pervasive adoption of cutting-edge technologies has the potential to reshape fundamental aspects of human life, influencing everything from interpersonal relationships to cognitive processes. Furthermore, recent studies underscore the need for an "omnicomprehensive" understanding of the intricate interplay between technology and wellbeing, as the convenience and efficiency afforded by these advancements are juxtaposed with concerns regarding privacy, mental health, and societal dynamics (Holdren, 2008; Meythaler et al., 2023; Robeyns, 2020).

Traditionally, literature in the realm of technology adoption has predominantly cantered on investigating factors influencing individuals' intentions to use new technologies, since the seminal works of Davis (1989) and so on.

2.1.1   *Previous and Seminal Studies Regarding New Technologies Acceptance*

The scrutinization of the issue of the new technological integrations, and its acceptance to use, and consequent behavioural responses in terms of individuals' intention to use such technologies, finds expression in the corpus of literature dedicated to the acceptance of software and, more broadly, information technology among its users. Predominantly explicated through the *Technology Acceptance Model* (TAM), as propounded by Davis (1989), this model has served as the theoretical foundation, subsequently undergoing augmentation in subsequent scholarly endeav-ours (Davis & Venkatesh, 1996; Davis & Wiedenbeck, 2001; Hackbarth et al., 2003; Karahanna & Straub, 1999; Roberts & Henderson, 2000). The TAM, rooted in the *Theory of Reasoned Action* posited by Fish-bein and Ajzen (1975), delineates behaviour as contingent upon the intention of the subject, shaped by attitudes towards the behaviour and subjective norms. Empirical investigations have consistently affirmed the TAM model's efficacy, delineating the independent influence of perceived usefulness and perceived ease of use on the acceptance of new technology (Davis & Venkatesh, 1996; Hackbarth et al., 2003; Kara-hanna & Straub, 1999; Roberts & Henderson, 2000). Furthermore, extant research underscores the paramount role of perceived usefulness in shaping attitudes (Davis, 1993; Venkatesh, 1999; Venkatesh & Davis, 2000).

Davis' seminal research posits that users may readily embrace a cumber-some tool that proves instrumental in their professional endeavours, contrasting with the reduced acceptance of an easy to use tool lacking utility for the designated task. Moreover, ease of use exerts an influence on perceived usefulness, with users ascribing greater utility to a facile tool (Davis, 1993). Within the milieu of factors influencing beliefs regarding information technology, the salience of self-efficacy perception emerges. As defined by Bandura (2006) and by Schwarzer and Luszczynska 2008, as an individual's confidence in successfully completing a specific task, self-efficacy varies with task complexity and past success or failure experiences. Venkatesh and Davis's (1996) exploration into the effects of self-efficacy towards computers and software usability on the perception of ease of use revealed a nexus between beliefs about system ease of use and subjects' perceptions of their ability to navigate the computer, both before and after practical engagement with the software. System usability became a salient consideration only post-initiation into the utilization of the new technology.

Recent scholarly inquiries have increasingly directed attention towards an internal marketing perspective, accentuating the impact of organi-zational context on new technology acceptance. Notably, the influence of social support and innovation climate is underscored, where support from colleagues, superiors, and the organization ameliorates work-related challenges, fosters emotional attachment, and propels individuals towards predefined objectives (Eisenberger et al., 1986). In times of organiza-tional transition, such as the introduction of new information technology, social support contributes to the alleviation of anxiety and stress among workers (Rhoades & Eisenberger, 2002). Certain scholars contend that successful innovation processes necessitate a climate conducive to the adoption and implementation of new technologies (Baer & Frese, 2003). The climate, defined as "workers' perceptions of the events, practices, and procedures and the types of behaviours that are rewarded, supported, and expected in a certain work setting" (Schneider, 1990, p. 384), assumes a pivotal role.

Nevertheless, given the contours of modern society and the evolving consumer landscape, concerted efforts and scholarly activities are imperative to explore potential variables influencing consumers' acceptance of new technologies, subsequently shaping their usage intentions and potential purchasing behaviours, mainly also focusing on the effects of their perceived wellbeing deriving from such usage.

2.1.2   Current State-of-the-Art and Use Cases Related to the Positive Integration of New Technologies in Crucial Industries

The integration of new technologies across various industries, such as healthcare, food waste management, music, tourism, smart mobility, and others, holds substantial promise not only for enhancing individual satisfaction and wellbeing but also for positively impacting society at large.

In healthcare, for instance, advancements in telemedicine and digital health platforms enable remote consultations and monitoring (Ekeland et al., 2010) or enable new forms of therapies as in the case of digital therapeutics (see Chapter 3), by finally enhancing access to healthcare services and improving patient outcomes (Senbekov et al., 2020). Similarly, technologies applied to food waste management facilitate efficient tracking, redistribution, and recycling of surplus food, thereby reducing waste and addressing food insecurity issues in communities (Benyam et al., 2021; Caianelli et al., 2015), also by leveraging on individuals' willingness to cooperate with the companies (e.g., as in Rizzo et al., 2023).

In the realm of music, streaming services and digital platforms have democratized access to diverse musical genres and facilitated personalized listening experiences, enhancing user engagement and cultural exchange (Brusila et al., 2022). Within tourism, technologies such as virtual reality (VR) and augmented reality (AR) are transforming travel experiences by offering immersive previews of destinations and historical sites, thereby enriching tourists' exploration and understanding of different cultures (Fennell, 2021; Marchegiani et al., 2024; Stankov & Gretzel, 2020).

Moreover, advancements in smart mobility (Paiva et al., 2021), including electric vehicles (Peters & Dütschke, 2014), autonomous transportation systems (Merfeld et al., 2019; Sestino et al., 2022), and ride-sharing platforms (Agatz et al., 2012), are promoting sustainable urban transportation solutions, reducing carbon emissions, and alleviating traffic congestion.

Furthermore, in education, the adoption of online learning platforms (Liu et al., 2020) and digital resources has democratized access to quality education worldwide (Blayone et al., 2017). For instance, students may now access lectures and resources and collaborate with peers remotely, which not only enhances learning flexibility but also accommodates diverse learning styles and needs. This accessibility promotes lifelong learning and skill development, empowering individuals to advance their careers and personal growth (Abuhassna et al., 2020). Work flexibility has been revolutionized by technologies that support remote work, virtual meetings, and collaborative tools as well (Boccoli et al., 2022, 2023; Suryadi et al., 2023). Employees can now balance work and personal responsibilities more effectively, reducing commuting stress and enhancing job satisfaction. This flexibility also fosters productivity and creativity, allowing individuals to work in environments that best suit their needs and preferences (Gajdzik & Wolniak, 2022; Hunter, 2019).

Overall, the integration of new technologies across these diverse industries underscores their potential to foster societal benefits.

Thus, by prioritizing innovation and responsible deployment, stakeholders may harness these technological advancements to promote inclusive growth, resilience, and wellbeing in both individual users and society as a whole.

2.1.3   *The Concept of Perceived Wellbeing*

The concept of individuals' perceived wellbeing, within the academic literature encompassing management, marketing, and consumer psychology and behaviour studies, may be defined as the subjective assessment and overall evaluation of an individual's satisfaction, happiness, and fulfilment derived from their consumption experiences and interactions with products or services.

Such a concept encompasses a holistic perspective that considers not only the functional benefits of a product or service but also the emotional, social, and psychological impacts on the individual. This multidimensional concept is influenced by various factors, including the quality of products, the accomplishment of needs and desires, social connections, and the alignment of consumption with personal values and goals.

For instance, perceived wellbeing, as measured by the Perceived Wellbeing Scale (PWB) developed by Reker and Wong (1984), refers to an individual's subjective evaluation of their overall psychological and physical state: Such a holistic concept, encompasses feelings of autonomy, positive relationships with others, personal growth, purpose in life, environmental mastery, and self-acceptance.

For instance, by focusing on the field of research related to consumers' psychology, scholars like Vohs and Baumeister (2016) emphasize the importance of understanding wellbeing beyond mere materialistic pursuits and highlight the psychological and emotional dimensions involved in consumer wellbeing.

In the field of marketing, researchers such as Kahneman and Krueger (2006) shed light on the role of emotional experiences in shaping consumer wellbeing, emphasizing the significance of positive emotional responses to products and services. Additionally, studies in consumer behaviour emphasize the role of hedonic experiences and the affective components of consumption in influencing individuals' perceived wellbeing (Hsee & Hastie, 2006).

Thus, by considering some previous literature on this domain, the concept of consumers' perceived wellbeing is a complex construct that integrates psychological, emotional, and social dimensions, as evidenced by the contributions from scholars in consumer psychology, marketing, and consumer behaviour studies. It reflects the subjective evaluation of the overall impact of consumption experiences on an individual's satisfaction and happiness.

2.1.4   Measuring Individuals' Perceived Wellbeing

The exploration and measurement of consumers' perceived wellbeing have been pivotal in the fields of consumer behaviour, marketing, and management.

Scholars have employed diverse methodologies and scales to shed light on the meaning of such a concept: In the realm of consumer behaviour, researchers have frequently utilized subjective self-report measures, employing surveys and questionnaires to gather individuals' self-assessments of their wellbeing in the context of consumption experiences. These measures often incorporate dimensions such as overall life satisfaction, affective states, and the perceived fulfilment of psychological needs. Notably, marketing scholars have developed specific scales to gauge consumers' perceived wellbeing in the context of their interactions with products and services.

For instance, the *Consumer Wellbeing Index* (CWI) proposed by Griskevicius et al. (2010) encompasses dimensions such as pleasure, arousal, and dominance, offering a comprehensive assessment of consumers' emotional and cognitive responses to consumption.

Moreover, the use of established psychological wellbeing scales, such as the *Flourishing Scale* (Diener et al., 2010), has become commonplace in examining the broader aspects of individuals' perceived wellbeing in marketing studies. Management scholars, meanwhile, have often adopted a holistic perspective, integrating organizational and environmental factors into the assessment of employees' wellbeing, recognizing the impact of workplace experiences on overall life satisfaction. Such consumers' perceptions have been also measured by employing the so-called PERMA model, as a consequence of the previously suggested models.

The PERMA model, developed by Martin Seligman (2011, 2018), would represent a comprehensive framework for understanding and measuring wellbeing, encapsulating five key elements in terms of: (1) Positive Emotion, (2) Engagement, (3) Relationships, (4) Meaning, and (5) Accomplishment. The PERMA model, by considering different meanings and dimensions, would seek to move beyond traditional conceptions of wellbeing solely as the absence of negative emotions and instead focus on the cultivation of positive aspects in individuals' lives. Indeed, by focusing on its component, (1) *Positive Emotion* refers to the experience of happiness and satisfaction; (2) *Engagement* pertains to the state of flow and absorption in activities; (3) *Relationships* emphasize the significance of social connections; (4) *Meaning* involves a sense of purpose and fulfilment; and (5) *Accomplishment* underscores the pursuit and achievement of goals (see Table 2.1).

In marketing and management studies, the PERMA model has been used in examining the factors contributing to consumer wellbeing and organizational success. Scholars have applied this model to investigate the

Table 2.1 The PERMA model and its components

Components of the model	Definition of the components
Positive Emotion (P)	The experience of happiness, joy, and overall positive affect. It involves cultivating positive feelings and emotions in individuals' daily lives
Engagement (E)	The state of being fully absorbed and immersed in activities leading to a sense of flow and optimal experiences. It emphasizes the importance of being actively engaged in individuals' pursuits
Relationships (R)	The quality and depth of social connections and relationships with others. This component highlights the significance of positive interactions and meaningful connections with family, friends, and communities
Meaning (M)	The sense of purpose, significance, and fulfilment derived from one's actions and contributions. It involves finding meaning and coherence in life's experiences
Accomplishment (A)	The pursuit and achievement of personal and professional goals. It encompasses a sense of mastery, competence, and successful outcomes in various domains of life

impact of positive emotions in different consumption experiences, e.g., in retail, food consumption, tourism, leisure, and so on (Doyle et al., 2016; Hollebeek & Belk, 2021; Rossetti et al., 2024), or to shed light on the role of consumers' engagement in brand loyalty (e.g., as in Hollebeek et al., 2014), and the influence of meaningful work in organizational contexts (e.g., as in Grant, 2008). The PERMA model, thus, serves as a robust theoretical foundation for exploring and enhancing wellbeing in diverse settings within the realms of marketing and management.

However, Butler and Kern (2016) also propose a coincide reasoning—together with a shorter scale—to measure the PERMA model, by proposing the so-called PERMA-Profiler. This short scale consists of 23 items, providing a quick yet comprehensive evaluation of an individual's overall wellbeing, that has been widely utilized in research across disciplines, including psychology, education, and management, contributing to the complete meaning of individuals' holistic wellbeing based on the PERMA model.

A Focus PERMA vs. PWB
Both the aforementioned Perceived Wellbeing Scale (PWB) developed by Reker and Wong (1984) and the PERMA model developed by Martin

Seligman (2011, 2018) are valid instruments aimed at assessing different dimensions of wellbeing but approach the concept from somewhat different perspectives.

To summarize and to clarify, while the PWB focuses on subjective evaluations across psychological and physical domains, including autonomy, relationships, personal growth, purpose in life, mastery, and self-acceptance, the PERMA model identifies five core elements of wellbeing in terms of Positive Emotions, Engagement, Relationships, Meaning, and Accomplishment. However, while both scales emphasize aspects of positive functioning and personal satisfaction, the PERMA model incorporates broader dimensions such as engagement and accomplishment, which are not explicitly measured in the PWB. Overall, the PWB provides a detailed assessment of perceived wellbeing across specific domains, whereas the PERMA model offers a holistic framework to understand and cultivate overall wellbeing based on these core elements.

Practically, the PWB may offer a straightforward and practical approach for experimental studies investigating aspects of wellbeing, since this scale is characterized by its clear and specific dimensions, including autonomy, relationships, personal growth, purpose in life, mastery, and self-acceptance, each measured succinctly through 17 items. If compared to the PERMA, this scale may facilitate efficient administration, minimizing participant burden. More importantly, the focused nature of the PWB aligns well with the objectives of experimental designs, and with the "holistic view" proposed in this book and may be useful—as shown in the next chapters to allow to precisely target and assess how interventions or treatments impact specific domains of wellbeing.

2.1.5 Goal of the Literature Review

A literature review about previous studies dealing with the issues of new technological integrations for improving individuals' wellbeing, and societal wellbeing is indispensable for a holistic comprehension of the technology adoption phenomenon, especially according to the recent paradigm of *Technology for the Humanity* (Kotler, 2021).

By narrowing the focus solely on adoption intentions, the literature risks overlooking the intricate dynamics between technology integration and users' overall psychological and emotional welfare. Therefore, a paradigm shift towards investigating the dimensions of wellbeing within the context of technology adoption is imperative to cultivate a more holistic and insightful discourse in this domain.

Building upon the outlined context, this literature review aims to shed light on the most extensively explored topics within the realm of new technology integration, specifically concerning their effects on individuals' wellbeing.

Formally, the present chapter, through the means of a systematic literature review would like to answer the following research questions:

RQ1. What are the primary subjects addressed in the existing literature dealing with the impact of new technological integrations on the wellbeing of individuals?

RQ2. Which areas of research show significant potential and merit further exploration within the context of the impact of new technological integrations on individuals' wellbeing?

2.2   MATERIALS AND METHOD

Following the systematic approach proposed by Tranfield et colleagues (2003) and similar to previous studies conducting a literature review (e.g., as for Guido et al., 2020; Sestino et al., 2020, 2022), this research conducts a critical review of experimental and review studies spanning the last decade (from January 2013 to December 2023).

The focus is on scholarly articles from international peer-reviewed journals investigating both new technologies and consumers' intention to use, together with the effect on their perceived wellbeing. To ensure a comprehensive search, a list of fourteen keywords also based on the aforementioned models was employed, together with various combinations of these terms. In doing so, three major business databases (i.e., Business Source Premiere and EconLit (EBSCO), ABI-INFORM Complete (ProQuest), and Scopus) were queried to identify articles in prominent management and marketing literature. The search targeted articles with specific terms in their titles, such as "technology", "new technologies", "intention to use", "wellbeing", "wellness", "positive emotion", "engagement", "relationship", "meaning", "accomplishment", "management", "marketing", "consumer", and "behaviour".

The selection process involved careful examination of identified articles for alignment with research objectives and subsequent content analysis through data extrapolation. A total of 112, documents were initially identified, and after successive screening processes, only 52 relevant contributions were selected for *in-depth* analysis, because strictly related to the topic under investigation.

These contributions were further synthesized, aligning with the consumer behaviour perspective, to stimulate discussions on designing effective management and marketing strategies based on emerging topics and future trends dealing with the effect of new technological integrations on individuals' wellbeing, by considering the technology that has been investigated in such contributions.

2.3   FINDINGS

2.3.1   *An Overview of the Findings from the Literature Review*

The analysis of the performed literature review reveals that while new technological integrations offer various benefits, concerns about privacy, security, ethical considerations, and the psychological impact on wellbeing are crucial aspects that need careful consideration.

To synthesize the findings, an exploration into the management of privacy and security concerns across technologies, as investigated by Wang et al. (2018), and Wu et al. (2017), brings to light concerns regarding data privacy, security, and the potential misuse of personal information. This emergent theme underscores the imperative need to assuage user apprehensions related to privacy and security in the adoption of new technologies.

Concerning Educational and Healthcare Applications of Immersive Technologies, an analysis of AR and VR, as exemplified by Chen and Lee (2019), Patel and Gupta (2017), and Huang and Wang (2019), showcases their influential roles in education and healthcare. This underscores a burgeoning focus on the educational and healthcare implications of immersive technologies. Exploring the issue of Human-AI Interaction and Ethical Considerations, as highlighted by Kim et al. (2020), Lee and Kim (2018), and Zhang and Li (2020), consistently underscores concerns and ethical considerations surrounding the integration of AI. It emphasizes the significance of delving further into the realms of human-AI interaction and ethical dimensions as a substantial emerging topic.

Regarding Psychological Wellbeing, studies investigating the impact of various technologies, such as VR experiences by Garcia et al. (2021)

and Park and Lee (2019), bring attention to the potential therapeutic applications of virtual reality. This emerging topic suggests a compelling need for additional research into the psychological effects of immersive technologies.

By now focusing on the type of technologies, in the realm of the *Internet of Things,* our literature review illuminates several studies on consumers' interactions with IoT devices and their impacts on usage intention and wellbeing (see Del Giudice, 2016; Sestino et al., 2020 for detailed reviews). Moreover, notably, Dong et colleagues (2017) uncovered a positive correlation between IoT usage and increased convenience, albeit with emerging concerns about data privacy. This aligns with Wang & Chang's assertion that smart objects' integration enhances user experience, positively influencing wellbeing through increased convenience and efficiency.

Regarding *Augmented* and *Virtual Reality*, early adopters' perceptions, as investigated by Chen & Lee (2019), reveal enhanced learning experiences with potential concerns about distraction effects. Similarly, Patel & Gupta (2017) explore the integration of virtual reality in healthcare, noting positive outcomes such as improved patient engagement. However, these immersive technologies necessitate careful consideration of potential drawbacks. Moreover, Garcia et al. (2021) demonstrate positive emotional states and stress relief associated with immersive VR experiences, highlighting potential psychological benefits. This aligns with findings emphasizing the positive impact of new technological integrations, such as AI-assisted services (Kim et al., 2020), on user satisfaction and perceived productivity, as evidenced by Liu et al. (2018) in the healthcare domain.

By leveraging the PERMA model and its sub-dimensions, findings consistently reveal that new technological integrations positively impact individuals' wellbeing across dimensions. Seligman et colleagues (2011, 2018) identify a positive correlation between IoT usage and key components of the PERMA model, suggesting that incorporating IoT and smart objects into daily life contributes to overall wellbeing. Coherently, literature (Liu et al., 2021) corroborates that IoT usage enhances positive emotions and engagement, positively influencing individuals' overall wellbeing.

Similar results have been confirmed by Kim et colleagues (2020), demonstrating that AI recommendations positively impact positive emotions and accomplishment. Wang and Chang (2016) show that smart objects positively influence positive emotions, engagement, and a sense of accomplishment, contributing significantly to overall wellbeing. Additionally, research focusing on virtual reality experiences (Zhang et al., 2019) demonstrates their positive effects on individuals' positive emotions and engagement, enhancing overall wellbeing.

In the context of *Artificial Intelligence*, Lee and Kim (2018) find positive engagement and accomplishment associated with AI-based tools, contributing to increased perceived wellbeing. AI-driven personal assistants, as explored by Park and Lee (2020), contribute to positive emotions and relationships, positively impacting users' overall wellbeing. Lastly, Chen et al. (2019) indicate that Augmented Reality positively influences positive emotions and engagement, emphasizing the potential benefits of incorporating AR technologies into daily life. Interestingly, positive emotions and engagement associated with virtual reality use, significantly contributing to users' overall wellbeing especially in terms of reduced due to the increased experiences of positive emotions (e.g., as in Kim et al., 2023).

2.3.2 A Focus on Technology Exploitation for Wellbeing Purposes, and Pivotal Industries

When closely focusing on the concept of wellbeing, the issue related to the integration of new technologies into consumers' experiences across various sectors such as health, music, tourism, and education has gained significant attention in recent research, particularly concerning its impact on consumer wellbeing (Robeyns et al., 2020). In the realm of tourism, McLean et colleagues (2023) investigated the influence of virtual reality (VR) tourism on consumers' subjective wellbeing, finding that immersive VR experiences can positively affect wellbeing by offering users an alternative means to engage with destinations, which can enhance their emotional and psychological state. Similarly, Wan and Onuike (2021) explored the potential of smart tourism innovations to foster sustainable tourists' wellbeing, by revealing that technology-driven experiences not only meet consumer demands for personalization and convenience but also contribute to a deeper sense of satisfaction and happiness when these technologies are used to promote sustainability. In the health sector, which by nature, above all others, is the one that must contribute to the wellbeing of individuals, the role of mobile health has been widely examined (see Eisenstadt et al., 2021 for a recent literature review on this topic).

To clarify, Antunes et colleagues (2022) conducted a study on Portuguese young adults' use of mental health apps, highlighting the gendered differences in app usage and their impact on wellbeing. They concluded that while mHealth apps have the potential to significantly improve mental health and wellbeing, their effectiveness is often mediated by user characteristics such as gender. Li and Chang (2021) further demonstrated the benefits of mHealth apps through their study on the usage of the mPower app for Parkinson's disease patients. Their findings underscore the importance of user engagement and personalized content in enhancing the efficacy of these apps, which ultimately contributes to better health outcomes. De Korte et al. (2018) also evaluated an mHealth app designed for workplace wellbeing, illustrating how such tools can support employees in managing stress and improving overall mental health when the apps are well-designed and more consumer centred.

When looking at the creative industries domain, e.g., in the context of music and education, the use of technology to enhance learning and wellbeing has also been explored (Himonides et al., 2022). For instance, to underline such relevance, Hu et al. (2021) conducted a qualitative study on university students' use of music for learning and wellbeing, suggesting that music streaming platforms and other digital tools can play a crucial role in students' emotional regulation and cognitive performance. Their research highlights the potential of music technology to support mental wellbeing and learning efficiency, especially when integrated thoughtfully into educational settings. The intersection of technology and wellbeing is also evident in the studies focused on digital mental health tools.

For instance, Inkster et colleagues (2018) examined the effectiveness of Wysa (https://www.wysa.com/), an empathy-driven conversational AI agent designed to support mental wellbeing. Their mixed-methods study revealed that users found Wysa to be a valuable tool for managing mental health challenges, particularly due to its empathetic design and personalized interaction. This reflects a broader trend towards using AI and IoT (Internet of Things) technologies to enhance wellbeing, as seen in the work of Navarro-Alamán et al. (2022) and Yang et al. (2018).

Navarro-Alamán et al. developed EmotIoT, an IoT system aimed at improving users' wellbeing by monitoring and responding to emotional states, while Yang et al. explored the application of long-term wearable social sensing technologies for mental wellbeing. Both studies underscore the potential of IoT and AI technologies to offer continuous, personalized support, thereby promoting sustained improvements in wellbeing.Thus, based on extant—and recent studies—the issue related to the integration of new technologies across various consumer domains has a profound impact on wellbeing, with the potential to enhance both mental and physical health, improve learning outcomes, and overall individuals' life quality.

These technologies, when designed with user needs and sustainability in mind, could significantly contribute to improved quality of life. However, the effectiveness of these technologies is often contingent upon factors such as individuals' engagement, personalization, and the consideration of demographic differences, which must be carefully addressed in future research and development.

Based on the above, and by considering the selected keywords and the precisely delineated scope focused solely on the analysis of the intention to use new technologies and their potential impacts on perceived wellbeing, the discerned outcomes have been systematically arranged in Table 2.2. This approach aims to enhance readability and provide a comprehensive overview of studies conducted in this specific domain.

Despite the aforementioned findings, some scientific contributions facing with both new technologies and wellbeing also focus on two important topics that cannot be neglected in terms of the use of new technologies for security purpose and for sustainable purpose, e.g., as in the case of twin transition-oriented strategies.

2.3.3   A Focus About Security and Sustainable Development

To integrate, in a broader sense, the emerging technologies employed for enhancing individuals' and collective wellbeing must also be considered for their application in national security (Akhgar et al., 2015; Lin et al., 2014).

To clarify, sometimes, technologies could be also used for unethical purposes (e.g., as for crypto for unethical goals and financing terrorism; Sestino et al., 2024; AI-driven disinformation campaigns manipulating public opinion; Bontridder & Poullet, 2021; cyberattacks targeting critical infrastructure vulnerabilities; Lehto, 2022; and so on); However, despite this negative exploitations, the "same" technologies may also play a crucial positive role, when pivotal in preventing such damages, e.g., as

Table 2.2 Synoptic table related to the major emerging studies

Authors	Setting	Type of research	Details	Findings
Lee et al. (2019)	Healthcare (older patients)	Qualitative	Review	• AR and VR can enhance physical and psychological wellbeing for elderly and older consumers; • Research is lacking on their social benefits and design challenges
Antunes et al. (2022)	Health & Wellness	Quantitative	Online survey with Portuguese adults	• Young adults use health and self-tracking apps more frequently than mental health apps, with those having children showing greater engagement with health and wellbeing technologies
Xu et al. (2021)	Music	Qualitative	Qualitative study conducted among a sample of 40 participants	• University students in China use music for learning and wellbeing, revealing its impact on physical health, social relationship, and emotional wellbeing
Wan and Onuike (2021)	Tourism	Quantitative	Sample of 43 participants (tourists)	• Personal technologies may enhance sustainable tourist wellbeing; • Smart tourism innovations balance hedonic and eudaimonic experiences (e.g., emotional components linked to wellbeing) enrich the overall satisfaction

(continued)

Table 2.2 (continued)

Authors	Setting	Type of research	Details	Findings
McLean et al. (2023)	Tourism	Quantitative	290 participants	• VR tourism positively impacts individuals' subjective wellbeing by enhancing psychological detachment and presence; • VR in tourism may positively affect both societal health benefits; • it also offers experience-related advantages for tourists and providers
Li and Chang (2021)	Health	Quantitative	Dataset collected from an mHealth app named mPower	• Professional diagnoses and high-performance scores boost mHealth app engagement; • Disease progression tends to reduce app usage
De Korte et al. (2018)	Health	Mixed method qualitative study	22 employees participated in interviews; 15 employees participated in three focus groups; 6 experts in a focus group	• Employees showed muted enthusiasm for the app, with varied insights from interviews, focus groups, and expert evaluations revealing different drivers, barriers, and concerns related to technology, user characteristics, context, privacy, and autonomy
Jones et al. (2014)	Gaming	Qualitative	Qualitative analysis	• Videogames may enhance mental health and wellbeing, since they promote positive affect, functioning, and social interactions

(continued)

Table 2.2 (continued)

Authors	Setting	Type of research	Details	Findings
Navarro et al. (2022)	Emotional control	Quantitative/ Explorative	Explorative study introducing a framework IoT-based	• IoT systems focused on detecting and predicting user emotions for forecasting future emotions and recommending activities on the basis of desired wellbeing goals
Yang et al. (2018)	Mental wellbeing	Quantitative	Trial Study	• IoT-based wearable social sensing platform integrating privacy-protected audio features, behaviour monitoring, and environmental sensing to assess long-term physical and mental health, may be useful (since the revealed correlations) to boost individuals' wellbeing
Inkster et al. (2018)	Mental wellbeing	Quantitative	Small sample of mental disease-affected patients	• High users of the app showed significantly greater mood improvement compared to low users; • users that found the app helpful and encouraging, perceive improved their wellbeing
Alqahtani et al. (2015)	National security purposes	Quantitative	Survey-based study	• Technology-related vulnerabilities (e.g., as for impact severity, control measures, and so on) to build a secure national infrastructure to prevent cyberattacks

for in the cases of terrorist attacks, safeguarding the population, finally thus improving individuals and societal wellbeing (see Mowery, 2009 for a seminal work). The integration of AI and big data analytics in counterterrorism efforts has been highlighted as essential in modern security strategies (Clarke & Knake, 2019). Thus, in a scientific discourse concerning the use and integration of new technologies into daily life, within the framework of a new "Digital Paradigm Shift", based on a new business DNA aimed at enhancing the wellbeing of individuals and societies (either directly or indirectly) this occurrence too cannot be overlooked.

2.3.4   A Focus on Twin Transition and Sustainable Development

The integration of new technologies in firms' core activities, not only enhances operational efficiency but also supports sustainable development (Silvestre & Țîrcă, 2019), e.g., through mechanisms such as twin transition and carbon neutrality.

In such a context *Twin Transition* refers to the concurrent advancement of digital transformation and green energy initiatives to drive sustainable development, by involving leveraging technology for economic growth while reducing carbon emissions and promoting societal wellbeing (Montresor & Vezzani, 2024; Ortega-Gras et al., 2021), carbon neutrality is referred to the goal of achieving a balance where the total carbon emissions are offset by actions such as reducing, reusing, or compensating, resulting in no net increase in atmospheric carbon dioxide (Wu et al., 2022). In this domain, new technologies, and specifically also new digital technologies, may facilitate the simultaneous advancement of digital and green transformations, promoting resource efficiency and reducing carbon footprints (Wang et al., 2021).

Furthermore, the adoption of innovative technologies enables businesses to achieve carbon neutrality by optimizing energy consumption and minimizing greenhouse gas emissions (e.g., Boulard et al., 2007). Consequently, these advancements could represent—on the basis of current best practice, and extant literature—a further example of the positive exploitation of new technologies in contributing to societal (and in this case, indirectly to individuals' wellbeing) by aligning with global sustainability goals and contribute to a more sustainable future.

Additionally, the role of new technologies plays a pivotal role in the development of emerging economies by fostering economic growth and improving quality of life, which cannot be neglected as well. Indeed, such new technologies today may also provide critical infrastructure for education, healthcare, and financial services, thereby accelerating socio-economic progress in developing countries (Stewart & James, 2019).

2.4   General Discussions and Conclusion

2.4.1   Overall Discussion

In this chapter, the objective was to shed light on the current streams of thought regarding some of the major studies and contemporary efforts in scientific literature related to the integration of new technologies. This focus particularly emphasized the analysis of the intention to use these technologies and their effects on wellbeing. The results of the conducted literature review shed light on thirty-four important contributions that have been discussed both by considering the type of technologies used, and the impacts on both intentions to use and perceived wellbeing. The current landscape of technological integration has prompted a burgeoning body of scholarly work investigating the effects on individuals' intention to use and perceived wellbeing. Recent studies, such as those by Wang and Chang (2021), and Kim et al. (2023), contribute significant insights to this discourse: The conducted literature review in this domain may thus be led to several potential theoretical contributions.

Firstly, we shed light on the relationship between individuals' techno-logical adoption intentions and the resultant impact on their wellbeing, providing a holistic perspective that encompasses both psychological and behavioural dimensions. Secondly, by synthesizing findings across diverse technological domains, the review facilitates the identification of common patterns and disparities, thereby contributing to the development of a unified theoretical framework that transcends specific technologies. Thirdly, the literature review aids in discerning the dynamic interplay between individual characteristics, differences, contextual factors, and the perceived benefits or drawbacks of technological integration, elucidating the multifaceted nature of the phenomenon.

2.4.2   Managerial Contributions

In terms of managerial implications, the literature review suggests several strategic considerations for organizations navigating the integration of new technologies. Firstly, recognizing the importance of user concerns surrounding privacy and security, managers should prioritize robust safeguards and transparent communication to foster user trust and mitigate apprehensions.

Secondly, understanding the varying impact of different technologies on educational and healthcare domains, organizations can tailor implementation strategies to align with the specific needs and objectives of these sectors.

Thirdly, acknowledging the ethical dimensions highlighted by studies on Human-AI Interaction, organizations should institute ethical guidelines and frameworks to guide responsible technological deployment. Finally, the positive correlations between wellbeing and certain technological integrations underscore the potential for organizations to position their technologies as enhancers of user satisfaction and overall wellbeing, thereby influencing consumer perceptions and preferences in a competitive market landscape.

2.4.3 Conclusion, Limitations, Final Remark and Other Chapters

While the conducted literature review proves to be a valuable resource, it is not without limitations. Notably, our examination has been confined to contributions to the English language, and furthermore, it has focused exclusively on the past decade. Recognizing these constraints, it is imperative to acknowledge the potential benefits of expanding the scope to encompass studies in other languages and extending the time span considered.

This approach would contribute to a more comprehensive understanding of the subject matter, incorporating diverse cultural perspectives and allowing for a better exploration of the historical evolution of technological integration's impact on intention to use and perceived wellbeing. In future research endeavours, a broader and more inclusive approach to the literature could enrich the depth and breadth of insights in this dynamic and evolving field.

To conclude, more importantly, by focusing on both a managerial and theoretical perspective, the literature review provides valuable insights for marketers and managers, emphasizing the need to recognize the distinctive individual differences among consumers that influence both the intention to use and the perception of wellbeing. These unique individual characteristics, as deeply underlined by the literature, may serve as crucial determinants in shaping the outcomes of technological integration efforts. Thus, understanding and acknowledging these typicalities is paramount for marketers seeking to tailor their strategies to diverse consumer segments and for managers navigating the complex landscape of technological adoption within their organizations.

Based on such intuitions, as explained in Chapter 1, the subsequent chapters will investigate deeper into these individual differences, exploring their implications on both the theoretical frameworks guiding research and the practical strategies employed by managers and marketers in the field.

Specialists' Perspectives. The Potential of New Technologies for Environmental Protection in Developing Countries

Environmental degradation represents one of the most pressing issues of the twenty-first century (Palmer, 2002; Warner et al., 2010). As the world grapples with the effects of climate change, pollution, and biodiversity loss, global ecosystems are degrading at an unprecedented level in human history, resulting in forest loss, land degradation and the extinction of species, all of which pose a severe threat to both the planet and people (Cardinale et al., 2012; Díaz et al., 2019).

Whilst representing a global phenomenon, these risks are magnified in developing countries, which are more vulnerable to the effects of environmental degradation and in which the unsustainable exploitation of natural ecosystems poses severe threats to the health and wellbeing of local communities (Busby et al., 2014; Nguyen et al., 2023). Developing countries are home to many of the world's most critical biodiversity hotspots (Fisher & Christopher, 2007), yet they frequently lack the resources and infrastructure needed to protect their natural wealth effectively (Bell & Russell, 2002). In this context, the rise of digital technologies offers a transformative opportunity for these nations to enhance environmental protection efforts, safeguarding ecosystems and promoting biodiversity, in line with the UNSDGs, particularly Goal 12 (Responsible Consumption and Production) and Goal 15 (Life on Land).

One of the primary environmental challenges in many developing countries is deforestation, driven by agriculture, logging, and urban expansion (Hoang & Kanemoto, 2021; Rudel, 2023).

New technologies, for instance remote sensing technology, and particularly satellite imagery, provide a powerful tool for monitoring these activities: Global Forest Watch (GFW), an open-source web application designed to monitor global forests in near real-time, integrates satellite-based sensors to measure global deforestation rates and detect and monitor illegal deforestation activities. Data provided by the GFW has been used by companies to track their supply chain, certifying their "no deforestation" commitments (Taylor et al., 2020; Nandasena et al., 2023).

Similarly, remote sensing technology can also be used to track wildlife populations (Kerr & Ostrovsky, 2003; Neumann, 2015; Katzner & Arlettaz, 2020). In Africa satellite imagery (Duporge et al., 2021) and drones (Wich et al., 2021) may be employed by researchers and conservationists to monitor elephant migratory patterns and identify vital habitats for protection for elephants and other keystone species.

New technologies may also play a vital role in enhancing agricultural practices in developing countries, leading towards a more sustainable use of land and agricultural resources (Khan et al., 2021). Agriculture remains a critical economic sector in most developing countries, and billions of humans depend on it for their economic subsistence and survival (Bruinsma, 2017). Nevertheless, unregulated usage of agricultural resources and the expansion of terrain destined for agricultural production has resulted in dramatic losses of forest cover, threatening biodiversity and accelerating issues of desertification and land degradation (Eswaran et al., 2019; Gomiero et al., 2011). The use of new digital tools for a smarter agriculture may tackle these issues, allowing for a better, optimized usage of existing resources and preventing the overexploitation of the natural environment to compensate for losses (García et al., 2020; Obaideen et al., 2022). The integration of smart irrigation devices and tools may prove to be particularly beneficial in developing countries, helping optimize irrigation and prevent excessive water usage (Nawandar & Satpute, 2019). Sangeetha et colleagues (2022) analysed the potential of implementing an IoT-based agricultural management system in rural India; the system used automated and IoT technologies for irrigation, temperatures forecast, and controlling air pressure. The results showed increased productivity and a decrease in energy consumption, as well as a reduction in total operating costs.

Lastly, new technologies may also help consumers make conscious choices when purchasing goods, learning about the ecological impact of products (Sestino & Sagona, 2024) and helping fight greenwashing practices by multinational companies (Rossi et al., 2024). In this context, the use of blockchain technologies to certify the origin and carbon footprint of goods across the entire supply chain may ensure greater accountability for firms operating in developing markets.

To summarize, the potential of new technologies for environmental protection in developing countries is substantial. Digital tools such as remote sensing and satellite imagery provide powerful means to monitor deforestation and track wildlife, aiding in the enforcement of conservation efforts. Innovations in agriculture, including smart irrigation and IoT-based management systems, can optimize resource use and prevent environmental degradation. Additionally, technologies like blockchain can enhance transparency in supply chains, helping consumers make informed choices and combat greenwashing.

Collectively, these advancements offer developing nations critical tools to safeguard their ecosystems, aligning with global sustainability goals and promoting biodiversity.

Alfredo Sagona, *International Business Developer*

References

Bell, R. G., & Russell, C. (2002). Environmental policy for developing countries. *Issues in Science and Technology, 18*(3), 63–70.

Bruinsma, J. (2017). *World agriculture: Towards 2015/2030: An FAO study*. Routledge.

Eswaran, H., Lal, R., & Reich, P. F. (2019). Land degradation: An overview. *Response to Land Degradation*, 20–35.

Busby, J. W., Cook, K. H., Vizy, E. K., Smith, T. G., & Bekalo, M. (2014). Identifying hot spots of security vulnerability associated with climate change in Africa. *Climatic Change, 124*, 717–731.

Cardinale, B. J., Duffy, J. E., Gonzalez, A., Hooper, D. U., Perrings, C., Venail, P., & Naeem, S. (2012). Biodiversity loss and its impact on humanity. *Nature, 486*(7401), 59–67.

Díaz, S., Settele, J., Brondízio, E. S., Ngo, H. T., Agard, J., Arneth, A., & Zayas, C. N. (2019). Pervasive human-driven decline of life on Earth points to the need for transformative change. *Science, 366*(6471), eaax3100.

Duporge, I., Isupova, O., Reece, S., Macdonald, D. W., & Wang, T. (2021). Using very-high-resolution satellite imagery and deep learning to detect and count African elephants in heterogeneous landscapes. *Remote Sensing in Ecology and Conservation, 7*(3), 369–381.

Fisher, B., & Christopher, T. (2007). Poverty and biodiversity: Measuring the overlap of human poverty and the biodiversity hotspots. *Ecological Economics, 62*(1), 93–101.

García, L., Parra, L., Jimenez, J. M., Lloret, J., & Lorenz, P. (2020). IoT-based smart irrigation systems: An overview on the recent trends on sensors and IoT systems for irrigation in precision agriculture. *Sensors*, *20*(4), 1042.

Gomiero, T., Pimentel, D., & Paoletti, M. G. (2011). Is there a need for a more sustainable agriculture?. *Critical Reviews in Plant Sciences*, *30*(1–2), 6–23.

Hoang, N. T., & Kanemoto, K. (2021). Mapping the deforestation footprint of nations reveals growing threat to tropical forests. *Nature Ecology & Evolution*, *5*(6), 845–853.

Katzner, T. E., & Arlettaz, R. (2020). Evaluating contributions of recent tracking-based animal movement ecology to conservation management. *Frontiers in Ecology and Evolution*, *7*, 519.

Kerr, J. T., & Ostrovsky, M. (2003). From space to species: ecological applications for remote sensing. *Trends in Ecology & Evolution*, *18*(6), 299–305.

Khan, N., Ray, R. L., Sargani, G. R., Ihtisham, M., Khayyam, M., & Ismail, S. (2021). Current progress and future prospects of agriculture technology: Gateway to sustainable agriculture. *Sustainability*, *13*(9), 4883.

Nandasena, W. D. K. V., Brabyn, L., & Serrao-Neumann, S. (2023). Using remote sensing for sustainable forest management in developing countries. In *The Palgrave Handbook of Global Sustainability* (pp. 487–508). Cham: Springer International Publishing.

Nawandar, N. K., & Satpute, V. R. (2019). IoT based low cost and intelligent module for smart irrigation system. *Computers and Electronics in Agriculture*, *162*, 979–990.

Neumann, W., Martinuzzi, S., Estes, A. B., Pidgeon, A. M., Dettki, H., Ericsson, G., & Radeloff, V. C. (2015). Opportunities for the application of advanced remotely-sensed data in ecological studies of terrestrial animal movement. *Movement Ecology*, *3*, 1–13.

Nguyen, T. T., Grote, U., Neubacher, F., Do, M. H., & Paudel, G. P. (2023). Security risks from climate change and environmental degradation: Implications for sustainable land use transformation in the Global South. *Current Opinion in Environmental Sustainability*, *63*, 101322.

Obaideen, K., Yousef, B. A., AlMallahi, M. N., Tan, Y. C., Mahmoud, M., Jaber, H., & Ramadan, M. (2022). An overview of smart irrigation systems using IoT. *Energy Nexus*, *7*, 100124.

Palmer, J. (2002). *Environmental education in the twenty-first century: Theory, practice, progress and promise*. Routledge.

Rudel, T. (2023). Population, development and tropical deforestation: a cross-national study. In *The Causes of Tropical Deforestation* (pp. 96–105). Routledge.

Sangeetha, B. P., Kumar, N., Ambalgi, A. P., Haleem, S. L. A., Thilagam, K., & Vijayakumar, P. (2022). IOT based smart irrigation management system for environmental sustainability in India. *Sustainable Energy Technologies and Assessments, 52*, 101973.

Sestino, A. & Sagona, A. (2024). Enhancing Green and Sustainable Consumption Trough The Use of Blockchain-based Digital Technologies: The Roles and Corporate Social Responsibility, and Consumer Environmental Self-Efficacy. Evidence from Sustainable Olive Oil and Wine Production. Accepted, in the *3rd Engage EU Conference, Responsible Production and Consumption: Current Issues and Advances towards SDG12*, Nov. 21–22, 2024, University of National and World Economy, Sofia, Bulgaria.

Taylor, R., Davis, C., Brandt, J., Parker, M., Stäuble, T., & Said, Z. (2020). The rise of big data and supporting technologies in keeping watch on the world's forests. *International Forestry Review, 22*(1), 129–141.

Warner, K., Hamza, M., Oliver-Smith, A., Renaud, F., & Julca, A. (2010). Climate change, environmental degradation and migration. *Natural Hazards, 55*, 689–715.

Wich, S. A., Hudson, M., Andrianandrasana, H., & Longmore, S. N. (2021). Drones for conservation. *Conservation Technology, 35*.

CHAPTER 3

The Crucial Role of Perceived Wellbeing in Mobile Health Technologies Adoption and Individuals' Positive Reactions: A Mediation Model

Abstract Mobile Health Technologies are transforming not only health-care but the entire process of healthcare delivery by enabling remote patient monitoring, continuous interactions, and more. In this context, the concept of the positive use of new technologies in the service of humanity is maximized, as it is situated within the healthcare setting, which is fundamentally aimed at restoring health and thereby oriented towards the wellbeing of individuals. Based on this premise in this chapter, through an exploratory research design based on an experiment conducted among a sample of 175 participants, we investigated the effect of integrating digital technologies (*vs.* the absence) in patients' monitoring and its impact on their positive reactions. The study, based on a 2×2 cell experiment, shed light on the positive effects of digital technology integration on both individuals' intention to use new technologies to follow therapies and engage in positive word-of-mouth. Importantly, we explored how individuals' perceived wellbeing resulting from the use of these technologies mediates (and explains) the aforementioned effects.

Keywords Smart health · Mobile health technologies · Digital therapeutics · Intention to use · Word-of-mouth · Perceived wellbeing

© The Author(s), under exclusive license to Springer Nature   45
Switzerland AG 2025
A. Sestino and L. Nasta, *The Digital Paradigm Shift for a New Business DNA*, https://doi.org/10.1007/978-3-031-76238-3_3

3.1   INTRODUCTION

The advent of new technologies is revolutionizing the healthcare sector comprehensively, impacting research, hospital processes, and, most notably, the delivery and enhancement of patient care services (Senbekov et al., 2020).

Advanced technologies, such as artificial intelligence, big data analytics, and telemedicine, are facilitating groundbreaking research, enabling the discovery of novel treatments and the optimization of clinical trials. In hospital management, these innovations streamline administrative workflows, improve operational efficiency, and reduce costs (Osipov & Skryl, 2021; Patil et al., 2022; Sestino et al., 2023).

Furthermore, the integration of cutting-edge tools in patient care is enriching the quality of services provided, offering more personalized, timely, and effective treatments, thereby significantly improving patient outcomes and satisfaction.

In this domain, *digital therapeutics* (DTx) and mobile health (mHealth) play a central role today. Formally, DTx refer to evidence-based therapeutic interventions driven by high-quality software programs to prevent, manage, or treat medical conditions (Dang et al., 2020; Hong et al., 2021; Sestino & D'Angelo, 2024). These interventions are designed to be used independently or alongside conventional treatments, often delivered via apps or online platforms (Fürstenau et al., 2023). mHealth, on the other hand, encompasses a wide range of mobile technology applications that support medical and public health practices through mobile devices, such as smartphones and tablets (Barton, 2012; Galetsi et al., 2023; Kosaraju, 2021).

As anticipated above, digital therapeutics include applications that provide cognitive behavioural therapy for mental health conditions, apps designed to help manage chronic diseases like diabetes through personalized medication reminders (Recchia et al., 2020), and programmes that offer tailored rehabilitation exercises for patients recovering from surgery or injury (Phan et al., 2023), e.g., also by leveraging on behavioural enablers such as the gamification (Sestino et al., 2023; Sestino & D'Angelo, 2024).

For instance, the app "reSET" provides therapy for substance use disorder (see Velez et al., 2021) while "Omada Health" offers a programme for diabetes prevention through lifestyle changes (Hong et al. 2021). In the realm of mHealth, examples include fitness trackers that monitor physical activity and vital signs (e.g., as in McConnell et al., 2018), telemedicine apps that enable remote consultations with health-care professionals (Waegemann, 2010), and medication adherence apps that remind patients to take their prescribed drugs.

These digital tools are enhancing patient engagement (Gybel Jense et al., 2024; Sestino et al., 2023), promoting adherence to treatment plans (Browne et al., 2018; Duthely et al., 2020), and facilitating contin-uous health monitoring (Bhavnani et al., 2016; Chatterjee et al., 2021), promoting individuals' socialization when affect by some disease, and increasing their responses to treatments (e.g., as for elderly patients; Sestino & D'Angelo, 2024; Shin et al., 2020) thus contributing signif-icantly to improved healthcare outcomes and patient empowerment.

In the healthcare context, the notion of sustainability, particularly regarding the social effects of business activities, is paramount (Rozen-blum & Bates, 2013). A healthcare enterprise, whether a clinic, hospital, care centres, or small medical practice, must meet the quintessential human need for health. The focus on social sustainability, understood as the pursuit of the original purpose of businesses, satisfying human needs, over their foundational objective of profit, is crucial.

Healthcare organizations are inherently tasked with the mission of enhancing and preserving human health, which aligns closely with the principles of social sustainability. This involves prioritizing patient well-being, providing equitable access to medical services, and fostering community health (Capolongo et al., 2016).

By integrating social sustainability into their operational strategies, healthcare enterprises can ensure that their activities not only generate economic value but also contribute positively to society. This approach demands a balance between financial performance and the ethical respon-sibility of meeting health needs, ultimately leading to more resilient and socially responsible healthcare systems.

Based on the above, the aforementioned new technological integra-tions, and applications such as digital therapeutics and mobile health can support the restructuring of business processes, contributing to the objec-tive of creating new patient services that are more precise, engaging, and supportive throughout all stages of the care pathway (Bhavnani et al., 2016; Chatterjee et al., 2021; Duthely et al., 2020; Gybel Jense et al., 2024; Sestino et al., 2023). These innovations exemplify how new tech-nologies contribute to social wellbeing, both for end users (patients) and, more broadly, for the community and society.

Moreover, the widespread adoption of these technologies promotes a more inclusive and efficient healthcare system, addressing disparities in access to care and empowering patients with information and tools to actively participate in their health management (Hong et al., 2021). In essence, the integration of digital therapeutics and mobile health into healthcare processes underscores the significant role of new technologies in enhancing social wellbeing, benefiting both individuals and society at large.

In this chapter we investigate the effect of new technological integration (*vs.* the absence of new technological integrations) on individuals' reactions, specifically in terms of intentions to follow the therapies and word-of-mouth, by importantly shedding light on the mediator role of their perceived wellbeing, deriving from such new technological usage in explaining such an effect.

3.2   THEORETICAL BACKGROUND

3.2.1   An Overview About Digital Therapeutics and Mobile Health Solutions

Digital therapeutics (DTx) and mobile health (mHealth) represent pivotal advancements in contemporary healthcare, driven by the integration of technology into medical practices. Digital therapeutics encompass software-based interventions that provide evidence-based therapeutic solutions to prevent, manage, or treat medical conditions (Dang et al., 2020; Hong et al., 2021). These interventions, often delivered through applications or digital platforms, are tailored to individual patient needs and are designed to complement traditional treatment methodologies (Fürstenau et al., 2023; Patil et al., 2022). mHealth, defined as the practice of medicine and public health supported by mobile devices, includes a broad array of services ranging from telemedicine consultations to mobile applications that monitor and manage patient health behaviours (Bhavnani et al., 2015; Duthely et al., 2020).

The literature underscores the efficacy of digital therapeutics in managing chronic conditions (e.g., for diabetes; Kaufman, 2019; chronic pain, Rogozinski et al., 2018; mental health; Carl et al., 2022; obesity prevention and intervention; Giannattasio et al., 2024; and so on), improving mental health, and facilitating behavioural changes. For instance, research indicates that digital cognitive behavioural therapy

(CBT) applications are effective in treating anxiety and depression, comparable to traditional "face-to-face" (*de visu*) therapy (Brezing & Brixner, 2022; Orsolini et al., 2024).

The hypothesis that the integration of digital therapeutics and technology, in general, can positively impact user intentions and reactions is well-supported by existing studies (Brezing & Brixner; Sestino et al., 2023). The use of digital platforms has been shown to increase patient adherence to treatment plans and enhance their overall engagement with healthcare services, and importantly stimulating positive behavioural responses in terms of intention to follow the therapies and overall final results (Kawasaki et al., 2022; Meyer et al., 2021).

This is attributed to the interactive and personalized nature of digital interventions, which cater to individual preferences and provide a sense of empowerment and control over one's health (Bulaj et al., 2021; Dang et al., 2021; Sestino et al., 2023; Sestino & D'Angelo, 2024). Furthermore, the convenience and accessibility of mHealth tools contribute to a more proactive approach to health management, fostering positive attitudes towards their use (Mazzeo & Zoccarato, 2020; van Kessel et al., 2023).

Thus, based on extant literature, the integration of digital therapeutics and mHealth into healthcare systems holds significant promise for improving patient outcomes and engagement. The evidence suggests that these technologies not only enhance the effectiveness of medical interventions but also positively influence patient behaviours and perceptions, shaping their positive reactions towards such new technological integrations (*vs.* its absence).

3.2.2 Perceived Usefulness, Ease of Use, and Wellbeing: A "Necessary" Clarification Perceived Wellbeing

In the academic discourse on technology adoption, it is essential to differentiate between perceived wellbeing and perceived usefulness (and ease of use). These constructs, while related, emerge from distinct theoretical frameworks and address different aspects of user interaction with technology.

More precisely, as the vision of this book suggests, the concept of *Perceived Wellbeing* refers to an individual's subjective evaluation of their quality of life and overall health status as influenced by technology (McDowell, 2010; Reker & Wong, 1984; Seligman, 2011). This concept is often derived from the fields of psychology and health sciences, where wellbeing encompasses physical, mental, and social dimensions (Seligman, 2011). Technologies that contribute to perceived wellbeing typically aim to enhance the user's life satisfaction, reduce stress, and improve health outcomes (Kari et al., 2017; Neves et al., 2023). For example, we may suggest that digital therapeutics and mHealth applications that support mental health, chronic disease management, and health behaviour modification are designed to elevate users' perceived wellbeing by providing personalized and accessible healthcare solutions.

Perceived Usefulness and Ease of Use: The TAM Model

On the other hand, *perceived usefulness* and *perceived ease of use* are constructs rooted in the so-called "Technology Acceptance Model" (TAM), a theoretical framework developed to explain user acceptance of information systems: In such a model, *perceived usefulness* is defined as the degree to which a person believes that using a particular technology will enhance their job performance or accomplish specific tasks; Conversely, *perceived ease of use* refers to the extent to which a person believes that using the technology will be free of effort (Davis, 1989; Venkatesh & Bala, 2008).

As Davis (1989) seminally suggests, the TAM posits that perceived usefulness and perceived ease of use are critical determinants of technology adoption and user satisfaction. According to the TAM, if a technology is perceived as useful and easy to use, individuals are more likely to accept and engage with it. These perceptions can significantly influence attitudes towards technology, shaping both initial adoption and continued use (Venkatesh & Davis, 2000).

While perceived usefulness and ease of use focus on the functional and operational aspects of technology, perceived wellbeing addresses the broader impact on an individual's quality of life. For instance, an mHealth app may be perceived as useful if it efficiently tracks health metrics and easy to use if it has an intuitive interface. However, its impact on perceived wellbeing would be evaluated based on how effectively it improves the user's overall health and life satisfaction.

3.2.3   The Mediator Role of Perceived Wellbeing in Shaping Individuals' Positive Reactions to New Technological Integrations

As for the issue related to the integration of new technologies in healthcare, such as digital therapeutics and mobile health, several scientific studies have provided substantial evidence demonstrating the effects of these technologies on perceived usefulness and ease of use. The (TAM) has been particularly instrumental in this regard, highlighting how perceived usefulness, and perceived ease of use, are critical determinants of technology adoption (Davis, 1989; Venkatesh & Davis, 2000).

For instance, studies on DTx have shown that when these technologies are perceived as useful in managing chronic conditions or improving mental health outcomes and are easy to use, they are more likely to be accepted and utilized by patients and healthcare providers alike (Carrera et al., 2023; Kim et al., 2022; Sestino et al., 2023; Sestino & D'Angelo, 2024; van Kessel et al., 2023).

However, to the best of the authors' knowledge, no studies have investigated the crucial role of perceived wellbeing deriving from the potential usage of these technologies. While perceived usefulness and ease of use address the functional and operational aspects of technology adoption, perceived wellbeing encompasses a broader evaluation of how these technologies impact an individual's overall quality of life and health status.

The crucial construct of *perceived wellbeing* derived from the use of technologies may significantly shape positive individuals' positive reactions and behaviour, such as intentions to use, adherence to therapy, and positive word-of-mouth.

When users experience improvements in their overall quality of life and health through technologies, they are more likely to develop favourable attitudes towards these tools (Lapid et al., 2015; Heinz et al., 2013; Jung, 2006). On the basis of previous seminal research indicating that perceived wellbeing can enhance user satisfaction and loyalty, leading to increased intentions to continue using the technology (Karahoca et al., 2018; Venkatesh et al., 2012), we can by extension postulate that such positive behaviour may be replied in positively accepting new technologies in healthcare, to improve the adherence to prescribed therapies, and precisely, in shaping individuals' intention (to use) new technologies to follow the therapy.

Furthermore, when individuals perceive substantial wellbeing benefits, they are more likely to share their positive experiences with others,
generating positive word-of-mouth (Fattahi et al., 2022; Gu et al., 2018).

Based on our reasoning, we finally postulate that the integration of new
technologies to support therapy (*vs.* absence) leads to greater intentions
to use the technology for following the therapy and generates positive
word-of-mouth. Moreover, since studies have shown that when individuals experience improvements in their overall quality of life and health
through technological interventions, they are more likely to develop
a positive attitude towards these tools, increasing their willingness to
use them consistently, and that the perceived wellbeing derived from
these technologies fosters a sense of satisfaction and loyalty, which, in
turn, encourages users to share their positive experiences with others,
promoting positive word-of-mouth, we suggest that the aforementioned
effect is explained by the perceived wellbeing attributed to the use of
these digital tools. To clarify, we predict that the perceived wellbeing is
a crucial mediator in the relationship between technology use in therapy
and the resulting behavioural intentions and communication behaviours.
Thus, formally, in this chapter we hypothesize that:

Hypothesis

> **H1a.** The digital technology integration (*vs.* absence) resulting as
> a DTx in supporting the therapy positively influences individuals'
> intention to use new technologies to follow such therapy.
> **H1b.** The digital technology integration (*vs.* absence) resulting as
> a DTx in supporting the therapy positively influences individuals'
> word-of-mouth.
> **H2a.** Individuals' perceived wellbeing acts as a mediator between the
> digital technology integration and intention to use.
> **H2b.** Individuals' perceived wellbeing acts as a mediator between the
> digital technology integration and word-of-mouth.

The proposed conceptual framework is shown in Fig. 3.1.

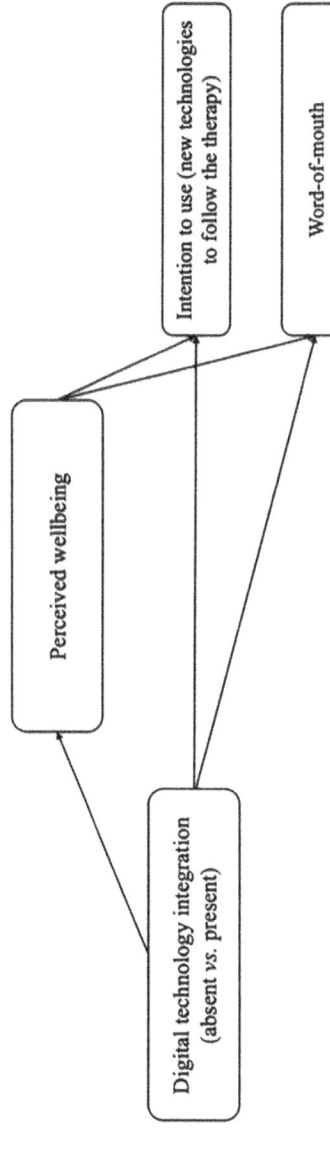

Fig. 3.1 The proposed conceptual model: The mediator role of individuals' perceived wellbeing

3.3   Materials and Methods

3.3.1   Sample and Materials

In this study, we manipulated the digital technology integration (absent *vs.* present) through two different scenarios related to the usage of digital therapeutics for cardiological purposes, and specifically for low-risk conditions (i.e., blood pressure monitoring).

The scenarios explained a traditional hypertension monitoring therapy that involves patients manually recording their blood pressure readings and reporting them during periodic medical appointments ("absent" condition"); In contrast, a digital therapy uses connected devices to automatically track and transmit blood pressure data to healthcare providers in real time, enabling continuous monitoring and timely interventions ("present" condition).

To confer empirical support to the hypotheses, a survey has been conducted among a sample of 175 participants aged between 21 and 75 years old ($M_{age} = 39.657$, $SD_{age} = 13.905$). Participants have been recruited next to some Italian hospitals in the Centre of Italy (next to the Rome area, i.e., Policlinico Gemelli Hospital, Umberto I Hospital); Participants have accessed the survey—prepared by using Qualtrics—either through a provided link or by scanning a QR code printed on a poster displayed in hospital areas.

Among the sample 84 of them declared to be male (48%), 86 of them declared to be female (86%), 2 of them non-binary (2%), while the residual 3 participants (3%) would not declare their gender. As for their education, while 77 of them (44%) declared to hold low or high school diploma, 42 of them (24%) declared to hold a B.Sc., 45 of them an M.Sc. (25,7%), 11 of them a Ph.D. (6.3%).

Moreover, as for their job, 86 of them were full employed (49.1%), 28 of them were part-time employed (16%), 15 of them were not employed (8.6%), 28 of them were students (16%) and finally, 18 of them were retired (10.3%). As for their while 72 of them (41.1%) declared to earn low than 20.000 euros, 57 of them (32.6%) declared to earn from 20,000 euros up to 39,000 euros, 29 of them (16.6%) declared to earn from 40,000 euros up to 59,999 euros (16.6%). Only 12 of them (6.9%) declared to earn from 60,000 euros up to 70,999 euros and only 2 of them declared to, respectively, earn from 80,000 euros up to 100,000 euros (1.1%), and more than 100,000 euros per year (1.1%).

3.3.2 *Questionnaire*

The questionnaire comprised three sections. After a welcome message, participants have been randomly assigned to two different scenarios within a two-cell experiment that manipulated the digital technologies absence *vs.* presence.

After being exposed to the stimuli, they reported their intention to use by using two items draw from drawn by Ajzen & (1975, 2000) (e.g., "I intend to use this tool to sustain my therapy"; $\alpha = 0.702$), and their perceived wellbeing adapted from Reker and Wong (1984) to operationalize and simplify Seligman's assumptions (2011) (e.g., "I could feel a sense of control over my life circumstances"; "I could feel satisfied with the quality of my life"; $\alpha = 0.681$). All the items were assessed on a seven-point Likert scale (1 = "Totally disagree", 7 = "Totally agree"). Finally, we collected the basic socio-demographics in terms of gender, age, education, job occupation, and income.

3.4 RESULTS

To test the conceptual model and hypotheses, we conducted a simple mediation analysis (Model 4), by using SPSS software, following the guidelines outlined by Hayes (2018).

The so-called "mediation analysis" is a statistical method used to examine the indirect effect of an independent variable on a dependent variable through one or more intervening variables, known as mediators (Hayes, 2018). In this specific study, the mediator helps explain the relationship between the independent and dependent variables, which in the examined case were the presence (*vs.* absence) of new digital technologies integrations on two independent variables, and thus on both intentions to use and word-of-mouth.

As aforementioned above, Hayes' approach provides a structured framework to assess whether the relationship between variables X (independent variable) and Y (dependent variable) is significantly influenced by the mediator Me.

Thus, by following our statistical analysis path, we launched the aforementioned Model 4 of PROCESS, by setting the digital technologies integration (coded as -1 = "absent"; 1 = "present") as the independent variable (Y), the perceived wellbeing acting as mediator (Me), and both individuals' intention to use, and then word-of-mouth as the two

Table 3.1 Simple mediation analysis: effects on intention to use

	b	SE	t	p
Step 1. Dependent variable: Perceived wellbeing (Me)				
Constant	4.094	0.105	38.867	0.000
Technological integration (absent *vs.* present) (X)	0.602	0.105	5.712	0.000
$R^2 = 0.159$, MSE $= 1.864$, $F(1, 173) = 32.625$ $p = 0.000$				
Step 2. Dependent variable: Intention to use (Y)				
Constant	0.819	0.223	3.673	0.000
Technological integration (absent *vs.* present) (X)	0.396	0.078	5.851	0.000
Perceived wellbeing (Me)	0.826	0.052	15.994	0.000
$R^2 = 0.705$, MSE $= 0.860$, $F(2, 172) = 205.906$, $p = 0.000$				
Direct Effect of X on Y				
	0.398	0.078	5.085	0.000

Notes. $N = 175$. Technological integration (independent variable, X); Perceived wellbeing (mediator, Me); Intention to use (dependent variable, Y)

independent variables (Y). The analysis has been performed firstly by analysing the effect of digital technologies integration on intention to use, through the effect of perceived wellbeing, and secondarily by analysing the effect of digital technologies integration on word-of-mouth because of the same mediator (perceived wellbeing). The results of our statistical analysis are reported in the tables in the next paragraphs (Tables 3.1 and 3.2).

3.4.1   Effects of Perceived Wellbeing on Intention to Use

Results immediately shed light on the direct effect of the presence of new digital technologies integration (*vs.* absence) on individuals' intention to use the new technologies to follow their therapy ($b = 0.398$, $t = 5.085$, $p = 0.000$).

Thus, we first regressed perceived wellbeing on the independent variable, and then we regressed individuals' intention to use on both the perceived wellbeing and the binary independent variable, that is the digital technologies integration.

The results showed that the presence (*vs.* absence) of new digital technologies in the therapeutical experience led to a higher level of perceived wellbeing ($b = 0.602$, $t = 5.712$, $p = 0.000$) and that perceived wellbeing, in turn, affected intention to use ($b = 0.826$, $t = 15.994$, $p =$

Table 3.2 Simple mediation analysis: effects on word-of-mouth

	b	SE	t	p
Step 1. Dependent variable: Perceived wellbeing (Me)				
Constant	4.094	0.105	38.867	0.000
Technological integration (absent *vs.* present) (X)	0.602	0.105	5.712	0.000
$R^2 = 0.159$, MSE $= 1.864$, $F(1, 173) = 32.625$ $p = 0.000$				
Step 2. Dependent variable: Word-of-mouth (Y)				
Constant	1.384	0.200	6.913	0.000
Technological integration (absent *vs.* present) (X)	0.830	0.070	11.861	0.000
Perceived wellbeing (Me)	0.836	0.046	18.061	0.000
$R^2 = 0.815$, MSE $= 0.692$, $F(2, 172) = 378.907$, $p = 0.000$				
Direct Effect of X on Y				
	0.830	0.070	11.861	0.000

Notes. N = 175. Technological integration (independent variable, X); perceived wellbeing (mediator, Me); word-of-mouth (dependent variable, Y)

0.000). However, when considering the intention to use as the dependent variable, the binary independent variable had a significant effect on it ($b = 0.396$, $t = 5.851$, $p = 0.000$).

3.4.2   Effects of Perceived Wellbeing on Word-of-Mouth

Similarly to the analysis related to individuals' intention to use as the independent variable, we then analysed the effects on individuals' positive word-of-mouth. Results of our statistical analysis firstly confirmed the direct effect related to the presence of new digital technologies integration (*vs.* absence) on individuals' positive word-of-mouth towards the new technologies usage to follow their therapy ($b = 0.830$, $t = 11.861$, $p = 0.000$).

Thus, by following the same procedure of above, we regressed perceived wellbeing on the independent variable, and then we regressed individuals' word-of-mouth on both the perceived wellbeing and on the binary independent variable, that is the digital technologies integration.

The results showed that the presence (*vs.* absence) of new digital technologies in the therapeutical experience led to a higher level of perceived wellbeing ($b = 0.602$, $t = 5.712$, $p = 0.000$) and that perceived wellbeing, in turn, affected word-of-mouth ($b = 0.836$, $t = 18.061$, $p = 0.000$).

However, to confirm, when considering the intention to use as the dependent variable, the binary independent variable had a significant effect on it ($b = 0.830$, $t = 11.861$, $p = 0.000$).

Thus, the results of the statistical analysis have confirmed our predictions, demonstrating that the integration of new digital technologies, such as DTx, has a positive and significant effect on final individuals' intention to use these technological tools to support their health recovery.

Furthermore, there is a positive word-of-mouth effect regarding the healthcare service experience, as well. Both the effects are explained by the mediating role of perceived wellbeing.

3.5   General Discussion and Conclusions

The integration of DTx and mHealth technologies into healthcare systems represents a significant shift in the medical landscape. This shift is not merely operational but extends to the very ethos of patient care and engagement. The findings from the present study highlight the crucial role of these technologies in enhancing patient outcomes, engagement, and overall satisfaction, reinforcing the theoretical framework provided by TAM.

The conducted experimental study enhances the traditional TAM by incorporating perceived wellbeing as a mediating factor, expanding the model's scope beyond just perceived usefulness and ease of use. This integration addresses a critical gap in the TAM framework, which historically emphasized operational and functional aspects of technology without considering the broader impact on user wellbeing.

Our findings are in line with recent research that also underscores the importance of perceived wellbeing in technology adoption within healthcare. For instance, Jeong et colleagues (2024), recently highlighted how DTx applications improve patient engagement and satisfaction by catering directly to individual health needs, thereby enhancing perceived wellbeing. Similarly, Alam et colleagues (2022) demonstrated that mHealth tools that offer personalized healthcare interventions are not only seen as useful but significantly contribute to the users' quality of life, thus reinforcing their continued use and advocacy.

Moreover, Sestino & D'Angelo (2024) have shown that the perceived ease of using these technologies correlates strongly with increased patient adherence and positive healthcare outcomes, potentially impacting patient perceptions of wellbeing. These studies validate our assertions about the critical role of perceived wellbeing in enhancing user satisfaction and loyalty, extending the implications of the TAM in contemporary digital healthcare contexts.

From a practical standpoint, these findings underline the importance for healthcare providers to prioritize technologies that enhance perceived wellbeing. Healthcare systems should consider adopting user-friendly and beneficial digital tools that not only aid in disease management but also contribute positively to the patient's quality of life. Implementing such technologies could lead to better patient adherence, reduced healthcare costs, and improved treatment outcomes.

Furthermore, the significant impact of perceived wellbeing on word-of-mouth suggests that satisfied patients are likely to become advocates for the healthcare services they receive, potentially increasing the adoption of these technologies through organic growth and patient referrals. Healthcare marketers and strategists can leverage this insight by promoting success stories and testimonials from satisfied patients who have benefited from these innovative technological solutions.

Future research should explore the longitudinal effects of DTx and mHealth on patient outcomes beyond the initial adoption phases. Long-term studies could provide insights into sustained engagement, adherence rates, and the evolution of patient attitudes towards healthcare technology over time.

Additionally, considering the diversity of digital health applications, studies could investigate specific types of DTx and mHealth solutions to identify which features or functionalities most effectively contribute to perceived wellbeing. This could help tailor digital health solutions to better meet the specific needs of different patient demographics or disease profiles.

Exploring cross-cultural differences in the adoption and impact of these technologies could also provide valuable insights, as cultural factors may influence perceptions of technology's usefulness, ease of use, and contributions to wellbeing.

Case Insights Box. The Case of AuReha: An Evidence-Based, AI-Powered, Digital Therapeutic for Neuromotor Rehabilitation

Rehabilitative therapies are essential for both acute and chronic conditions, as they help restore functional abilities, reduce deficits, prevent complications and slow the disabling effects of chronic conditions. In addition to the clinical benefits, they significantly improve the quality of life of patients and their caregivers.

In recent years the demand for rehabilitation services has increased and is expected to grow due to the aging population and the spread of chronic diseases. However, the increase in demand encounters several difficulties in traditional clinical practice, such as scarcity of resources, complexity in patient management, lack of evidence for treatment plans, limitations in access to services and difficulties in maintaining adherence to home rehabilitation plans.

DigitalRehab s.r.l., an innovative startup founded in 2021, fits into this context by dealing with research, development and commercialization of Digital Therapeutics (DTx) for neuromotor rehabilitation, as therapeutic interventions via software with demonstrable clinical benefits. The company is specialized in the implementation of connected, accessible, affordable, evidence-based and AI-enhanced solutions through the development of fully integrated and certified medical devices for the prescription by clinicians and asynchronous monitoring of digital rehabilitation therapies performed in a domestic environment, maintaining high standards of safety and compliance. DigitalRehab team reflects the commitment to merge therapeutic pathways and digital innovation to create high-quality solutions, thanks to clinical, engineering, and business expertise. Its method is based on working with a participatory approach for all the involved stakeholders to understand and meet end users' needs.

DigitalRehab's main solution to overcome the criticalities mentioned above is AuReha, an integrated system of three main components: a sensorized shirt which connects to a serious games application for patient use and a web platform for therapists. The shirt integrated with inertial sensors captures the movements, connecting to the app to allow patients to perform domestic rehabilitation in engaging virtual environments. The algorithm personalizes the targets of the sessions real time according to patients' performance, to provide a customized therapy and to allow a gradual recovery. In addition, the patient is supported by a virtual coach which gives instructions, biofeedback and scores. At the end of the session, the software provides functional and motor parameters shown in the web platform, used by the therapist for asynchronous monitoring: therapists can easily access the patients profile, set the rehab journey and evaluate parameters of the domestic sessions, considering the progress and the needs of the patients. Data analysis and applications of machine learning-based logics allow the identification of patterns and trends to support clinical decisions, promoting scientific research in the definition of treatment models and accurate therapeutic recommendations.

With AuReha, geographic distance is overcome in favor of increased sustainability, clinical outcomes, and the quality of life for patients and caregivers. This connected care model is a core value for patients since it promotes supervised self-management in the therapeutic plan, allowing active involvement and improving satisfaction during recovery. AuReha promotes adherence to therapy using engaging scenarios, a customized therapy and additional support by the virtual coach. The concept of adherence and the effective use of the solution, which both enable its prescription and reimbursement, are closely linked to the awareness and skills of the end users. DigitalRehab recognizes the importance of a strategic approach, in which demand, supply and ecosystem for the integration of the solution are coherent with each other, overcoming the digital literacy gap of end users by supporting the training and engagement of new patients and experts through structured courses, certification training and users' focus groups.

Camilla Larini, *CTO DigitalRehab*; Silvia Sciamanna, *COO DigitalRehab*; Giuseppe Recchia, *CEO DigitalRehab*; & Eugenio Luciani, *Business Advisor DigitalRehab*

Case Insights Box. "Virtual Reality for Real Care" a New Approach to Treatment, Training, and Prevention
VRFORCARE advocates for the **ethical use of emerging technologies** (AI, VR, AR, and the Metaverse) in **medical, social,** and **preventive fields.** The initiative aims to develop reliable and validated tools that can significantly enhance treatment pathways in psychiatry, address pathological addictions (both substance and behavioral), prevent workplace accidents, and promote individual wellbeing.

Numerous international meta-analyses have demonstrated the efficacy of VRFORCARE's approach. By leveraging the power of experiential processes through VR headsets, subjects can undergo emotionally intense and "dangerous" experiences in a virtual setting rather than in reality. This allows them to learn and become aware of their resources and potential risks in a controlled, virtual environment, always under the supervision of expert professionals.

VRFORCARE does not propose a cure but rather implements the **most effective tools available** to clinicians for treatment and prevention. A key strength of VRFORCARE is its commitment to avoiding standardized, generic solutions. Instead, it co-designs and co-creates tailored solutions with clients through a customized 'training' pathway to address specific needs.

VRFORCARE offers applications in two major areas: Immersive Virtual Reality with varying levels of interaction, and Conversational Assistants powered by Artificial Intelligence. Among its value propositions, VRFORCARE relevant products are:

1. **DRIM (DRugs IMmersion)**—An immersive, highly interactive environment simulating a party scenario. Participants actively engage and can choose to accept or decline various offers from other party attendees. The VR scenario utilizes real actors, not avatars, enhancing the sense of presence;

2. **Zen Garden**—A moderately interactive environment with visual and auditory stimuli, allowing participants to explore a Zen garden and choose relaxing spots;

3. **CHIARA** and **ALTEA**—Two Conversational Assistants: CHIARA, is trained for three specific tasks in the area of eating disorders (DCA) such as a) Monitoring the food diary post-discharge from DCA treatment; b) Conducting follow-ups after psychotherapeutic and/or psychopharmacological treatments; and c) Performing basic screenings to assess the presence of psychopathology and/or pathological addictions. ALTEA focuses on supporting patients undergoing treatment for cocaine addiction. It monitors progress and assists during crises. These tools are available 24/7, providing therapists with valuable information through patient-avatar interactions.

An immersive VR application focusing on workplace safety is under development. This aims to provide subjects with simulated dangerous or deadly experiences and educate them on appropriate safety measures.

Piergiovanni Mazzoli, *Scientific Director*, VR-For-Care

The Crucial Role Experienceable Positive Emotions in Shaping Positive Reactions to AI-Based Digital Tools. Evidence from Music Services for Wellness Purposes

Abstract The rapid advancement of AI has transformed how listeners discover and interact with music, especially through AI-driven streaming services that offer personalized recommendations. Despite music's significant role in shaping emotions and enhancing mood, there is limited research on how AI tools' perceived ease of use (PEOU) and perceived usefulness (PU) impact positive emotions and trust. This study explores these relationships by surveying 242 music streaming users and applying Structural Equation Modelling-Partial Least Squares analysis. The findings show that both PEOU and PU significantly influence perceived positive emotions, which in turn affect trust in AI-based tools. These insights link technological acceptance with emotional outcomes, highlighting the importance of emotional responses in fostering trust and satisfaction with AI. Practically, these results can guide the design of more user-friendly and emotionally engaging recommendation systems. Future research should examine demographic factors and the long-term effects of sustained AI interactions on emotions and trust in music streaming services.

Keywords AI-based music recommendations · Perceived ease of use · Perceived usefulness · Positive emotions · Individual trust

© The Author(s), under exclusive license to Springer Nature
Switzerland AG 2025
A. Sestino and L. Nasta, *The Digital Paradigm Shift for a New Business DNA*, https://doi.org/10.1007/978-3-031-76238-3_4

4.1   INTRODUCTION

The rapid advancement of AI technology has profoundly impacted various facets of our daily lives, including how we consume and interact with music. In 2023, a significant 79% of music fans were aware of AI's capabilities, demonstrating the widespread recognition and integration of AI in the music industry (International Federation of the Phonographic Industry, 2023).

The integration of AI in music streaming services has revolutionized the way listeners discover new music, with sophisticated algorithms recommending tracks tailored to individual tastes and preferences. This seamless and personalized music consumption experience promises not only to enhance user satisfaction but also to influence emotional wellbeing (Celma, 2010; Kostrzewa, 2024). Given the pivotal role music plays in shaping emotions and enhancing mood, understanding how AI-based digital tools in music streaming services affect perceived positive emotions and trust in these tools becomes essential (Assuncao et al., 2022; Koo, 2022).

The adoption of AI in music streaming services has garnered significant attention in recent research. Studies have explored various dimensions, such as the technological capabilities of recommendation algorithms, user satisfaction with personalized playlists, and the broader implications of AI on the music industry (Schedl et al., 2018). For instance, previous research highlights that recommendation algorithms, driven by AI, can significantly improve user engagement by providing a more personalized listening experience (Schedl et al., 2017). Moreover, the perceived accuracy and relevance of these recommendations are crucial factors that contribute to the overall satisfaction of users with music streaming services (Deldjoo et al., 2024).

Despite the wealth of research on the technological and user satisfaction aspects, there is a noticeable gap in understanding the emotional impacts of AI-based recommendations. Specifically, how PEOU and PU of these AI tools influence users' experienceable positive emotions, and in turn, their willingness to trust these digital tools, remains underexplored. Emotional responses to music are integral to human experience, affecting not only immediate mood but also long-term mental wellbeing (De Witte et al., 2022; Juslin & Västfjäll, 2008). Notably, in 2023, 71% of people state that music is important to their mental health, underscoring the significant role music plays in emotional wellbeing (International Federation of the Phonographic Industry, 2023). Hence, a deeper investigation into this emotional dimension could provide valuable insights into optimizing AI-based music recommendation systems for enhancing user trust and wellbeing.

Our approach aims to fill this gap by proposing a model that links the PEOU and PU of AI-based digital tools with perceived experienceable positive emotions, and subsequently, with the willingness to trust these tools. By examining this model within the context of music streaming service consumption, we aim to elucidate the pathways through which AI recommendations influence user emotions and trust.

To this end, our study formulates the following problem statement: How do the perceived ease of use and perceived usefulness of AI-based digital tools in music streaming services affect users' experienceable positive emotions, and how do these emotions subsequently influence their willingness to trust the AI tools?

To investigate this problem, we conducted a comprehensive empirical study involving a survey of 242 music listeners who use a popular music streaming service that employs AI algorithms for music recommendation. We employed Structural Equation Modelling-Partial Least Squares analysis to investigate these relationships. Our analysis revealed that both PEOU and PU significantly affect perceived experienceable emotions, and these emotions, in turn, influence the willingness to trust AI-based digital tools.

The outcomes of this research are expected to contribute to the existing literature on AI in digital media consumption by providing new insights into the emotional and trust-related aspects of AI tools. Theoretically, this research bridges a significant gap by linking the technological acceptance of AI tools with emotional and trust outcomes in the context of music consumption (Sundar, 2020; Xu et al., 2023). Moreover, the findings could have practical implications for developers and marketers of AI-based music streaming services, guiding them in designing more user-friendly and emotionally engaging recommendation systems that foster user trust and satisfaction.

By enhancing our understanding of these dynamics, stakeholders can better leverage AI to not only meet user expectations but also to enhance their emotional wellbeing, ultimately fostering a more trusting relationship with AI technologies.

4.2   THEORETICAL BACKGROUND

4.2.1   The Role of AI in Music Streaming Services

The integration of AI in music streaming services has revolutionized the way listeners discover and engage with music. Historically, music recommendation systems have evolved from basic collaborative filtering techniques to sophisticated AI-driven algorithms that can process vast amounts of user data to deliver personalized music recommendations. These algorithms leverage various methodologies, including collaborative filtering, content-based filtering, and hybrid models, to predict user preferences accurately (Bobadilla et al., 2013; Celma, 2010).

Collaborative filtering, for instance, analyses patterns in user behaviour to recommend tracks that similar users have enjoyed. This method can be further divided into user-based and item-based collaborative filtering. User-based collaborative filtering recommends items liked by similar users, while item-based collaborative filtering recommends items that are similar to those the user has previously liked (Koren et al., 2009). On the other hand, content-based filtering assesses the characteristics of songs—such as genre, tempo, and instrumentation—to suggest similar ones. This approach relies heavily on the metadata of the music and the analysis of audio signals to create feature vectors for comparison (McFee et al., 2012).

Hybrid models combine these approaches to enhance recommendation accuracy and user satisfaction by mitigating the limitations inherent in each method. For instance, Netflix and Spotify use hybrid recommendation systems to leverage the strengths of both collaborative and content-based filtering (Bennett & Lanning, 2007; Velankar & Kulkarni, 2022). These systems can handle sparse data more effectively, improve recommendation diversity, and reduce the cold-start problem where new users or items have little interaction data (Anderson et al., 2020).

The benefits of AI-driven music recommendations are manifold. They provide a highly personalized listening experience, which not only improves user engagement but also increases user satisfaction by consistently delivering relevant and enjoyable music (Deldjoo et al., 2020; Kostrzewa, 2024). This personalized experience is achieved through continuous learning from user interactions, enabling the system to refine its recommendations over time. Reinforcement learning techniques, for example, allow recommendation systems to adapt to user feedback dynamically, thereby improving the relevance of future recommendations (Afsar et al., 2022).

Major music streaming platforms such as Spotify, Apple Music, and Pandora have successfully employed AI to create dynamic playlists and recommendation features, significantly influencing user listening habits and preferences. Spotify's Discover Weekly and Daily Mix playlists, for example, are well-known for their ability to introduce users to new music that aligns with their tastes (Anderson et al., 2020). These platforms use deep learning techniques to analyse not only user listening history but also social media trends and music metadata to enhance the accuracy of their recommendations (Wang et al., 2023).

The perceived accuracy and relevance of these AI-generated recommendations are crucial factors contributing to the overall satisfaction of users, as they feel more connected to the music selected for them, fostering a deeper engagement with the platform (Maslowska et al., 2022). Studies have shown that user satisfaction with music recommendations can significantly influence their continued use of the streaming service and their willingness to pay for premium features (Hariri et al., 2012). Moreover, the ability of AI to continuously adapt to changing user preferences helps maintain long-term user engagement and loyalty (Hesmondhalgh et al., 2023).

4.2.2 Emotional and Trust Implications of AI Recommendations

Emotional responses to music are integral to human experience, affecting not only immediate mood but also long-term mental wellbeing (Colin et al., 2023; De Witte et al., 2022).

Music may evoke a wide range of emotions, from joy and excitement to nostalgia and relaxation, thereby playing a critical role in enhancing listeners' quality of life (Eseadi & Ngwu, 2023; Juslin & Västfjäll, 2008). In this context, the PEOU and PU of AI-based music recommendation tools play significant roles in shaping users' emotional responses and their willingness to trust these digital tools. PEOU refers to the degree to which a user believes that using a particular system would be free of effort, while PU is the degree to which a user believes that a system enhances their performance (Venkatesh & Davis, 2000).

When users find AI tools easy to use and beneficial, they are more likely to experience positive emotions during music consumption, such as joy, relaxation, and emotional connection (Carole et al., 2024; Silvester and Kurian, 2023).

The emotional impact of AI-based recommendations is further amplified by the personalized nature of these tools. Personalized music recommendations can significantly enhance the emotional experience by aligning song choices with the user's current mood or situational context (Jin et al., 2019). For example, mood-based playlists or situational recommendations (e.g., workout playlists, relaxing evening music) can create a tailored emotional journey for the listener, thereby increasing the perceived value of the AI tool (Gao, 2022).

The ability of AI to adapt to individual preferences and provide emotionally resonant content fosters a sense of connection and satisfaction, which are crucial for building trust in technology (Kang & Lou, 2022).

Empirical studies have shown that positive emotional experiences fostered by AI-based recommendations can enhance users' trust in these technologies. Trust is a crucial factor in technology adoption, particularly in AI applications where transparency and predictability are often concerns (Assunção et al., 2022). Trust in AI systems is built through consistent and positive user experiences, where the technology reliably meets or exceeds user expectations (Madadipouya & Chelliah, 2017). When users consistently encounter music that resonates with their preferences and enhances their emotional wellbeing, their trust in the AI system increases, leading to greater acceptance and continued use of the technology (Koo, 2022).

This relationship underscores the importance of optimizing AI algorithms not only for accuracy and relevance but also for emotional resonance. By prioritizing user emotions in the design of AI-based recommendation systems, developers can create more engaging and trustworthy digital tools. Emotional resonance may be enhanced by incorporating user feedback mechanisms, contextual awareness, and adaptive learning capabilities into the recommendation algorithms (Wang et al., 2018). For instance, by understanding the user's context (e.g., time of day, activity, mood), AI can suggest music that is more likely to elicit positive emotional responses (Ben Sassi & Ben Yahia, 2021). This approach not only improves the user experience but also builds a stronger, trust-based relationship between the user and the technology.

Moreover, transparency in AI operations can further bolster trust. When users understand how recommendations are generated and feel assured that their data is used ethically, they are more likely to trust and engage with the AI system (Sundar, 2020). Providing explanations for why certain songs are recommended can demystify the AI process and make users feel more in control of their music experience (Afchar et al., 2022). Consequently, trust, once established, can lead to increased user satisfaction and loyalty, creating a virtuous cycle of positive interactions and enhanced trust.

Thus, based on the previous literature and the above discussions, the following hypothesis is proposed:

Hypothesis

> **H1**. PEOU of AI-based digital tools (recommender systems) posi-
> tively impacts perceived experienceable positive emotions.
> **H2**. PU of AI-based digital tools (recommender systems) positively
> impacts perceived experienceable positive emotions.
> **H3**. Perceived experienceable positive emotions positively impact the
> willingness to trust AI-based digital tools (recommender systems).

The proposed conceptual framework is shown in Figure 4.1.

4.3 Materials and Method

4.3.1 Sample and Materials

The questionnaire was distributed via Prolific, targeting frequent music streaming service users to ensure a diverse and representative dataset of experienced users. A total of 242 participants answered the survey. This sample size was sufficient for Structural Equation Modeling (SEM) analyses, as recommended by Kline (2015). Data was checked for missing values, distribution, and outliers using SPSS (version 26), with no significant issues identified.

To reduce social desirability bias and common method variance (Podsakoff et al., 2003), participant anonymity and confidentiality were emphasized, and participation was voluntary and uncompensated. Questions for independent and dependent variables were separated to minimize bias.

SPSS was used for descriptive statistics, reliability analysis, and to evaluate demographics and internal consistency of constructs. SmartPLS 3.0 was employed for Partial Least Squares (PLS) analysis to assess the study

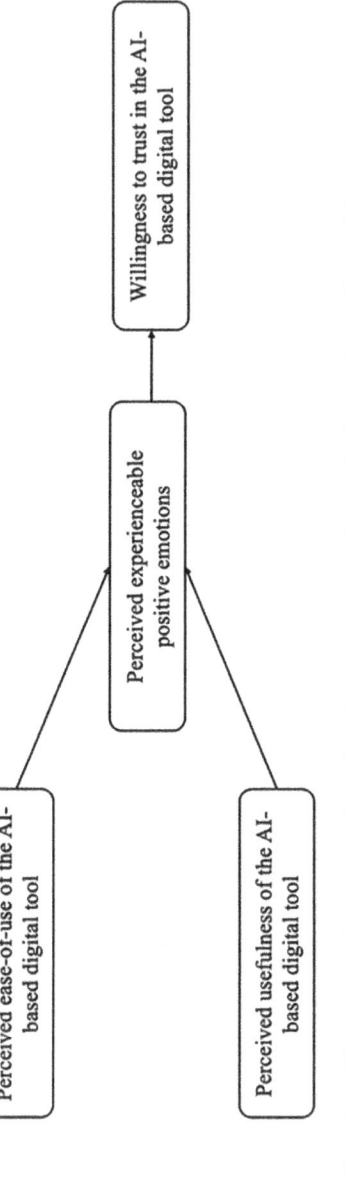

Fig. 4.1   The proposed conceptual model: The crucial role of perceived experienceable positive emotions

model. Following the standard two-step SEM analysis, the measurement model (validity and reliability) and the structural model were examined. A bootstrapping method with 5000 resamples was applied to evaluate the significance of path coefficients and loadings (Hair et al., 2019).

Among the sample, 143 participants declared to be male (59.1%), 95 participants declared to be female (39.3%), 3 participants identified as non-binary (1.2%), and 1 participant preferred not to disclose their gender (0.4%).

Regarding their age, 6 participants (2.5%) were under 18, 123 participants (50.8%) were between 18 and 24 years old, 54 participants (22.3%) were between 25 and 34 years old, 25 participants (10.3%) were between 35 and 44 years old, 18 participants (7.4%) were between 45 and 54 years old, 6 participants (2.5%) were between 55 and 64 years old, 9 participants (3.7%) were between 65 and 74 years old, and 1 participant (0.4%) was 75 years or older.

As for their education, 8 participants (3.3%) had less than a high school diploma, 69 participants (28.5%) were high school graduates, 9 participants (3.7%) held an associate degree, 92 participants (38.0%) had a bachelor's degree, 44 participants (18.2%) had a master's degree, 9 participants (3.7%) held a professional degree, 5 participants (2.1%) had a doctorate, and 6 participants (2.5%) had other educational qualifications.

Regarding their subscription status, 189 participants (78.1%) were premium members of music streaming services, while 53 participants (21.9%) were free users.

In terms of time spent listening to music, 48 participants (19.8%) listened for less than 1 hour per day, 87 participants (36.0%) listened for 1–2 hours per day, 44 participants (18.2%) listened for 2–3 hours per day, 31 participants (12.8%) listened for 3–4 hours per day, and 32 participants (13.2%) listened for more than 4 hours per day.

4.3.2   Questionnaire

To evaluate the theoretical model outlined in Figure 4.1 and to test the associated hypotheses, a survey instrument was developed using established constructs from the literature. Participants were asked to rate their agreement with each statement using a 7-point Likert scale ranging from 1 ("Totally disagree") to 7 ("Totally agree").

PEOU and PU of the AI-based recommender system were measured using a 3-item scale and a 5-item scale, respectively, from Davis (1989).

These scales assess how user-friendly and accessible the AI-based digital tool is perceived to be, as well as its perceived usefulness. For PEOU, items included statements such as "It's easy to use the recommender system" and "The recommender system is understandable and clear" (α = .74). For PU, items included statements such as "By using the recommender system, I improve my ability to accomplish the tasks I have in mind" and "By using the recommender system, I save time for the tasks I have in mind" (α = .89).

Perceived experienceable positive emotions were measured with a 9-item scale adapted from Sarafim et al. (2019) and Tarrant et al. (2000), including statements like "Music helps me through difficult times" and "Music helps me maintain a good mood" (α = .84).

Willingness to trust the AI-based recommender system was measured with a 2-item scale adapted from the concept of behavioural intention by Fishbein and Ajzen (1977). Items included "I intend to trust this recommender system in the future" and "I will trust this recommender system in the future" (α = .94).

Finally, basic socio-demographic information was collected, including gender, age, education, job occupation, and data on the usage of music streaming services.

4.4   Results

4.4.1   Measurement Model

First, we assessed the convergent validity of the model, as shown Table 4.1.

This assessment was conducted using factor loadings, Composite Reliability (CR), and Average Variance Extracted (AVE). According to Table 4.1, all standardized factor loadings exceeded the recommended threshold of 0.5 (Hair et al., 2009). The composite reliability values, which indicate how well the construct indicators represent the latent construct, were all above the suggested value of 0.7. Additionally, the AVE values, which reflect the amount of variance in the indicators attributable to the latent construct, surpassed the recommended threshold of 0.5 for all constructs except perceived experienceable positive emotions. Despite this, the CR value for this construct was well above the 0.7 threshold, allowing it to be accepted (Hair et al., 2019).

Table 4.1 Convergent validity

Construct	Indicator	Item	Loading	Alpha	CR	AVE
PEOU	PEOU1	It's easy to use the recommender system	.692***	.737	.844	.644
	PEOU2	The recommender system is understandable and clear	.799***			
	PEOU3	Using the recommender system requires minimum effort	.613***			
PU	PU1	By using the recommender system I improve my ability to accomplish the tasks I have in mind	.768***	.893	.920	.697
	PU2	By using the recommender system I save time for the tasks I have in mind	.814***			
	PU3	By using the recommender system I enhance the effectiveness of the tasks I have in mind	.849***			
	PU4	Using the recommender system makes it easier to accomplish the tasks I have in mind	.805***			
	PU5	The recommender system is useful in accomplishing the tasks I have in mind	.722***			
POS_EMO	POS_EMO1	Music helps me through difficult times	.701***	.844	.879	.448

(continued)

Table 4.1 (continued)

Construct	Indicator	Item	Loading	Alpha	CR	AVE
	POS_EMO2	Music relaxes me when I am stressed	.782***			
	POS_EMO3	Music reduces loneliness	.657***			
	POS_EMO4	Music relieves boredom	.613***			
	POS_EMO5	Music helps me be creative	.563***			
	POS_EMO6	Music helps me express my feelings	.574***			
	POS_EMO7	Music facilitates thinking	.559***			
	POS_EMO8	Music helps me maintain a good mood	.565***			
	POS_EMO9	Music makes me enjoy life	.684***			
BITRUST	BITRUST1	I intend to trust the recommender system in the future	.730***	.94	.810	.681
	BITRUST2	I will trust the recommender system in the future	.608***			

Note ***All standardized factor loadings are significant at the 0.01% level

Next, we evaluated discriminant validity, which examines how distinct the measurements are from other variables. This was evidenced by low correlations between the target measure and other constructs. Henseler et al. (2015) recommend using the heterotrait-monotrait (HTMT) ratio of correlations based on the multitrait-multimethod matrix. Table X presents the results of the HTMT ratio of correlations test for discriminant validity. According to the first criterion, discriminant validity may be compromised if the HTMT value exceeds 0.85 (Kline, 2015). However, as shown in Table 4.2, all values were below 0.85, indicating satisfactory discriminant validity.

Table 4.2 Discriminant validity

	IBTRUST	POS_EMO	PEOU	PU
IBTRUST				
POS_EMO	.645			
PEOU	.359	.242		
PU	.217	.209	.561	

4.4.2   Structural Model

In this study, a resampling technique with 5,000 samples was employed, following Hair and colleagues (2009), to assess the structural model.

Results shows that PEOU of AI-based recommender system significantly impact perceived experienceable positive emotions ($\beta = 0.146$; t-value = 2.066; $p < 0.05$), thus supporting our first hypothesis.

Similarly, PU of AI-based recommender system positively and significantly influences perceived experienceable positive emotions ($\beta = 0.122$; t-value = 1.692; $p < 0.1$), thus confirming the second hypothesis.

Lastly, perceived experienceable positive emotions positively and significantly impacts on the willingness to trust the AI-based recommender system ($\beta = 0.440$; t-value = 8.982; $p < 0.001$), thus supporting our last hypothesis.

Moreover, PEOU and PU of the AI-based recommend system accounted for 49.3% of the variance in respondents' attitudes towards the products. Attitude explained 27.3% of the variance in behavioural intention, while behavioural intention explained 48.5% of the variance in word-of-mouth (Table 4.3).

Table 4.3 Structural model

Hypothesis	Description	Beta	t-value	Decision
H1	PEOU → POS_EMOT	.146*	2.066	Supported
H2	PU → POS_EMOT	.122⁺	1.692	Supported
H3	POS_EMOT → BITRUST	.440***	8.982	Supported

4.5   GENERAL DISCUSSION AND CONCLUSIONS

The current study investigates the evolving dynamics of AI integration within music streaming services, specifically focusing on how AI-driven recommendation systems influence user emotions and trust. Our research bridges the gaps identified in prior studies by linking TAM with emotional outcomes, a relatively underexplored area in the context of music consumption.

The findings of this study contribute to the theoretical landscape by extending the traditional TAM framework, introducing perceived experienceable positive emotions as an intervening factor between PEOU, PU, and trust in AI systems. This integration adds an additional layer to our understanding, suggesting that emotional responses significantly contribute to the relationship between user interface design and trust in technology. Our results support and expand upon the work of Venkatesh and Davis (2000), who highlighted the direct impacts of PEOU and PU on user acceptance and satisfaction. By incorporating emotional responses into this model, our research highlights how AI-enhanced systems in music streaming not only satisfy functional needs but also play a crucial role in emotional wellbeing (Juslin & Västfjäll, 2008; De Witte et al., 2022).

This also resonates with the concept of affective computing as introduced by Picard (2000), which refers to the design and development of systems and devices that can recognize, interpret, process, and simulate human emotions. The core idea behind affective computing is that by enabling machines to understand and respond to the emotional states of human users, interactions can become more intuitive, effective, and human-like. This alignment with the principles of affective computing demonstrates how technological interfaces that cater to emotional needs can enhance user satisfaction, trust, and engagement, thereby reinforcing the overall impact of digital technologies on wellbeing.

Our study could contribute to the ongoing dialogue about the transformative role of AI in enhancing user experiences on digital platforms. By linking AI's technical capabilities with emotional connectivity, we echo and expand upon Sundar's (2020) observations regarding how technological interfaces shape user perception and trust. The integration of AI in music streaming services transcends basic functionality; it redefines the user experience by creating a more intuitive and emotionally resonant interaction with music. This is pivotal, as Celma (2010) and Kostrzewa (2024) suggest, because music is inherently linked to emotional experience and personal identity.

AI-driven recommendation systems do not merely suggest tracks based on listening habits but analyse a multitude of user data to personalize music in a way that resonates with the current emotional state and situational context of the listener.

This capability demonstrates an advanced understanding of user needs and preferences, fostering a deeper emotional connection between the user and the music they encounter. For instance, by analysing the tempo, lyrics, and melody of music in conjunction with user feedback, AI can offer music that matches or alters the listener's mood, enhancing their overall experience.

This emotionally intelligent curation is crucial for sustaining user engagement and satisfaction. As users experience consistently positive interactions with AI recommendations that seem intuitively aligned with their emotional needs, their trust in the platform grows. This trust is not just based on the functional success of the algorithms but also on the emotional support they perceive the platform provides.

Given the importance of emotional resonance in user interactions, our results suggest that developers and designers of AI systems should prioritize the emotional aspects of their algorithms. As music streaming services become an integral part of daily life, the emotional intelligence of these platforms could distinguish them in a saturated market, enhancing user retention and attracting new users seeking a more personalized and emotionally supportive experience.

Future research could explore several avenues to build upon the findings of this study. One area of interest could be the exploration of different demographic variables such as cultural background and technological familiarity, and their impact on the relationship between AI tool use and emotional outcomes. Additionally, longitudinal studies could provide insights into how sustained interactions with AI influence user emotions and trust over time.

Another promising area for further research is the exploration of negative emotional responses to AI recommendations. While our study focused on positive emotions and trust, understanding the conditions under which AI recommendations might evoke negative emotions could provide a more balanced view and guide improvements in AI system designs.

Case Insights Box. Moving Towards a Deeper Understanding of Music Technology and Emotions

How do we connect with sound?

What roles can sound play in cognition and emotion?

How can sound affect our moods?

How does technology impact our experience of music?

One goal of the entertainment industry is to connect emotionally with audiences, and the medium most used to strengthen this connection is technology applied to sounds. Knowledge of music, acoustics, computer science, and psychology allows music technologists to create compelling soundscapes in various contexts. As such, sound has a vital role as a narrative medium to evoke emotional responses. Technology acts as an invisible instrument: even though its role is not always evident, songs and sounds in films would only resonate globally with it.

I am a dedicated educator and practitioner in music technology. At NYU Abu Dhabi, I hold the position of Associate Professor of Music Technology and have worked in the music and film industry for over 20 years, witnessing the rapid changes in technology and how it affects the well-being of people. In my journey as a technology practitioner, I have noticed that personal experiences and cultural context shape our musical tastes and how we should apply technology to connect with an audience emotionally. From the music we are exposed to during childhood to the cultural norms and trends of the time, these elements play a significant role in determining the types of music we enjoy.

Our brains also respond to music in complex ways, involving multiple areas associated with emotion, memory, and pattern recognition. What is fascinating is that the brain releases dopamine, a neurotransmitter associated with pleasure, when we listen to music we enjoy, reinforcing our preference for specific songs or genres, but only if all the sonic elements have been purposely worked to engage emotionally with us. This is strongly associated with a crucial technological role called mixing. The emotion-inducing power of music has been an impetus for conversation, research, and curiosity for many centuries. Listening to music is part of our daily lives. This aspect of technology started to affect the creation and production of music. Today, it is an integral part of the recording arts and can influence our perception of a musical piece immensely. While numerous academics are researching the aspects of performing and recording music, mixing music has yet to be explored much. As technology progressed throughout the years, mixing became an art form tied to technology and our emotional connection.

During the past 20+ years of working as a mixing engineer, I have observed a powerful bond that connects music, mixing, and cognition and the power that music has to unfold emotions in the listener. Several other mixing engineers describe acknowledging and listening to the emotions in a piece of music as essential to creating a strong product. Sonic quality has become one of the most important factors when it comes to music. Every year, record companies issue digitally remastered versions of classic albums that allegedly sound better than the originals, and that is because technology gave us the power to perfect the sound. A good mix can sharpen the emotional message of a musical piece, make it more appealing to the listener, and boost commercial success. Mixing involves harmonizing multiple audio elements, encompassing a range of instruments, into a unified whole. Mix engineers can be viewed as "sonic artists" who enhance a musical piece's emotional impact.

Matteo Marciano,

Associate Professor of Music Technology New York University

Mixer, Sound Designer

From Augmented Reality to Life Satisfaction: The Role of Gamification in Cultural Heritage Experiences

Abstract The cultural heritage sector is increasingly adopting innovative technologies like augmented reality (AR) and gamification to enhance visitor experiences. AR overlays digital information onto the physical world, creating immersive experiences, while gamification applies game-design elements to make learning more engaging. This study examines the impact of perceived usefulness (PU) and perceived ease of use (PEOU) of AR technology on the enjoyment of gamified experiences, and how this enjoyment influences individual engagement and perceived learning effects during visits to archaeological sites. Data from 164 participants were analysed using Partial Least Squares Structural Equation Modelling. The findings show that both PU and PEOU significantly enhance enjoyment in AR experiences, which in turn drives higher engagement. This increased engagement positively affects perceived learning outcomes, which contribute to overall life satisfaction. The study highlights the importance of designing AR technologies that are both useful and easy to use to maximize enjoyment, engagement, and educational value in cultural heritage settings.

Keywords Augmented reality · Gamification · Cultural heritage · Individuals' engagement · Life satisfaction

© The Author(s), under exclusive license to Springer Nature Switzerland AG 2025
A. Sestino and L. Nasta, *The Digital Paradigm Shift for a New Business DNA*, https://doi.org/10.1007/978-3-031-76238-3_5

81

5.1   INTRODUCTION

In recent years, the integration of digital technologies into everyday experiences has revolutionized various domains, with AR emerging as a pivotal tool in enhancing user engagement and satisfaction. According to a report by BIS Research (2018), the global AR market is expected to reach $198 billion by 2025, reflecting its growing relevance and adoption. Cultural heritage sites, with their rich historical and educational value, represent an ideal canvas for the application of AR technologies. The use of AR in these settings has the potential to significantly enhance the visitor experience, transforming how individuals interact with and perceive cultural heritage.

Furthermore, this enhanced experience may contribute to broader aspects of life satisfaction by fostering a deeper connection to cultural heritage and promoting educational and emotional fulfilment. By making historical information more accessible and engaging, AR can help visitors form meaningful connections with the past, leading to a heightened sense of cultural appreciation and personal enrichment.

Traditional methods of presenting information at cultural heritage sites often fail to fully engage modern audiences, particularly younger generations accustomed to interactive and immersive digital experiences. Previous research has demonstrated that AR can address these challenges by overlaying digital information onto the physical environment, creating an interactive and immersive learning environment. Studies have shown that AR can significantly enhance visitor engagement and learning outcomes by making historical information more accessible and engaging (Damala et al., 2008; Economou & Tost, 2011; Fanini et al., 2023; Fenu & Pittarello, 2018; Ghouaiel et al., 2017; Graziano & Privitera, 2020; Jung et al., 2016).

Gamification, the application of game-design elements in non-game contexts, has also been recognized as an effective strategy to increase user engagement and motivation. Elements such as avatar selection, artifact collection, and rewards and tokens can transform a passive visit into an active and enjoyable experience, and overall, digitalization is deeply contributing in the cultural heritage industries also supporting as a means to reclaim the heritage that is being lost or destroyed (Massi & D'Angelo, 2022).

Previous studies (Deterding et al., 2011; Koivisto & Hamari, 2019; Houtari & Hamari, 2012; Sailer et al., 2017) highlight that gamification can enhance intrinsic motivation and enjoyment, leading to higher levels of engagement and satisfaction. Despite the growing body of research on AR and gamification, there remains a gap in understanding how these technologies can synergistically integrate to enhance the visitor experience at cultural heritage sites and how this enhanced experience can contribute to broader life satisfaction.

This paper positions itself at the intersection of AR technology, gamification, and visitor engagement, proposing a model that links these elements to overall life satisfaction. Our approach focuses on understanding how PU and PEOU of AR technology influence the enjoyment derived from gamification elements, which in turn affects the level of engagement. This engagement is hypothesized to enhance the perceived learning effect, ultimately leading to greater life satisfaction. This model builds on TAM proposed by Davis (1989), which emphasizes the importance of PU and PEOU in technology adoption and extends it to encompass the role of gamification and its impact on engagement and learning in the context of cultural heritage site visits.

The research question guiding this study is: How do perceived usefulness and perceived ease of use of augmented reality technology influence the enjoyment of gamification elements, and how do these factors together affect engagement, perceived learning, and overall life satisfaction in the context of visiting cultural heritage sites?

By addressing this question, we aim to provide insights into the design and implementation of AR applications for cultural heritage sites, highlighting the potential of these technologies to enhance visitor experiences and contribute to broader life satisfaction.

We aim to conduct this study by testing our proposed model through a survey-based study. We designed a scenario in which 164 participants were asked to imagine using an AR device to visit an ancient Roman amphitheatre, a typical cultural heritage site. We employed Partial Least Squares Structural Equation Modelling to test the relationships among the variables of the study.

From a theoretical perspective, this research contributes to the understanding of how AR and gamification elements interact to influence visitor engagement and satisfaction.

By extending TAM to include gamification and its effects on engagement and perceived learning, this study provides a more comprehensive framework for examining technology adoption in cultural heritage contexts. Recent studies by Hsu and Chen (2018) and Rauschnabel et al.

(2019) further support the relevance of integrating AR and gamification to enhance user experiences in various settings.

From a practical perspective, the findings of this research can inform the design and implementation of AR applications for cultural heritage sites. By understanding the factors that enhance visitor engagement and satisfaction, cultural heritage managers and technology developers can create more effective and enjoyable AR experiences. This can lead to increased visitor numbers, longer visits, and higher overall satisfaction, thereby supporting the preservation and appreciation of cultural heritage. Moreover, the insights gained from this study can be applied to other contexts where AR and gamification can be used to enhance user experiences, such as museums, educational institutions, and tourism.

5.2   Theoretical Background

5.2.1   Technology Acceptance Model for Augmented Reality Applications

TAM, developed by Davis (1989), is a widely recognized framework for understanding technology adoption. TAM asserts that PU and PEOU are the primary factors influencing users' acceptance of technology. In the context of cultural heritage sites, TAM is particularly relevant as it helps to understand how visitors interact with AR technologies.

Recent studies have highlighted the importance of PU and PEOU in the successful implementation of AR applications in cultural heritage settings. For instance, a study by Cheng et al. (2023) demonstrated that visitors' perceived usefulness of AR applications significantly enhances their engagement and satisfaction during museum visits. This is echoed by Marasco et al. (2018), who found that AR applications, by providing detailed and interactive content, substantially improve the perceived value of cultural heritage experiences. Similarly, the ease of use of AR applications positively influences users' intention to use these technologies, thereby improving their overall experience (Jung al., 2016). This is further supported by Tussyadiah et al. (2018), which showed that PEOU directly impacts users' attitudes towards AR, making them more likely to engage with the technology.

Additionally, empirical research has shown that AR can make cultural heritage sites more attractive to younger audiences, who are typically more familiar with and receptive to different new technologies (Nasta &

Pirolo, 2021; tom Dieck & Jung, 2017). This demographic often values seamless and intuitive interfaces, which aligns with the TAM's emphasis on PEOU. When AR applications are designed to be user-friendly and intuitive, they can cater to the preferences of these tech-savvy visitors, enhancing their overall experience and satisfaction.

The relevance of TAM in AR applications for cultural heritage sites is also evident in the work of Lim et al. (2024), who investigated the impact of AR on tourist experiences. Their study revealed that PU and PEOU are crucial in shaping tourists' attitudes towards AR, which in turn affects their overall satisfaction and intention to revisit.

This reinforces the idea that the successful implementation of AR in cultural heritage sites hinges on making the technology both useful and user-friendly.

Moreover, a comprehensive study reviewing various educational settings found that AR's PU and PEOU significantly contribute to positive learning outcomes and engagement (Akçayır & Akçayır, 2017). These findings can be extrapolated to cultural heritage sites, where educational aspects are paramount. The ease with which visitors can use AR applications to access and understand historical information enhances their learning experience, making their visits more enriching and enjoyable.

5.2.2 *Enhancing Visitor Engagement Through Gamification*

Gamification, the incorporation of game-design elements in non-game contexts, has been recognized as an effective strategy to boost user engagement and motivation.

According to Seligman (2011), enjoyment and engagement are critical components of wellbeing. Activities that are intrinsically enjoyable and engaging contribute significantly to an individual's overall happiness and life satisfaction. In cultural heritage sites, gamification can transform a passive visit into an interactive and enjoyable experience.

For example, Koivisto and Hamari (2019) found that gamification elements, such as rewards and challenges, enhance users' intrinsic motivation, leading to higher engagement levels. Similarly, Sailer et colleagues (2017) and Xi and Hamari (2019) emphasize that gamification can increase user satisfaction by making the experience more enjoyable and immersive. By integrating gamification into AR applications, cultural heritage sites can provide visitors with a more engaging and enjoyable experience, fostering a deeper connection to the cultural content and enhancing overall visitor satisfaction.

Recent studies have further explored the impact of gamification on user engagement. Hamari et al. (2014) conducted a comprehensive review of gamification literature and concluded that game-design elements such as points, leaderboards, and badges significantly increase user engagement and motivation.

Their findings are corroborated by studies in various contexts, including education (Dicheva et al., 2015), health (Sestino et al., 2023), and workplace settings (Seaborn & Fels, 2015).

In the specific context of cultural heritage sites, gamification can serve multiple purposes. Firstly, it can make the learning process more enjoyable. Nofal et al. (2020) found that gamified experiences in museums lead to higher levels of engagement and learning, as visitors are more likely to interact with exhibits and absorb information when game elements are involved. This enhanced engagement not only makes the visit more enjoyable but also deepens the visitor's connection to the cultural content.

Secondly, gamification may attract a broader audience, particularly younger visitors who are accustomed to interactive and digital experiences. For instance, a study by Cesário and Nisi (2023) demonstrated that gamification in museum settings significantly increased the participation of younger audiences. The study showed that elements like quests and virtual rewards were particularly effective in engaging this demographic.

Moreover, gamification may encourage repeat visits and longer engagement durations as well: Coherently, Bugeja and Grech (2020) found that visitors who participated in gamified activities at cultural heritage sites were more likely to return and spend more time exploring the site compared to those who did not participate in such activities. This suggests that gamification not only enhances the immediate visitor experience but also fosters long-term engagement and loyalty.

Incorporating gamification into AR applications at cultural heritage sites can also facilitate social interaction among visitors. Fitz-Walter et al. (2011) highlighted that gamified AR experiences often include social elements, such as team challenges or shared quests, which can enhance the social aspect of the visit. This social interaction can further enhance the overall visitor experience by adding a layer of collaborative enjoyment and shared discovery.

5.2.3   Impact of Augmented Reality on Learning Outcomes and Life Satisfaction

The perceived learning effect is a crucial factor in evaluating the impact of AR and gamification on visitor experiences at cultural heritage sites. Effective learning in informal settings, such as museums and cultural heritage sites, is often influenced by the perceived relevance and engagement of the content (Ozdemir et al., 2018). AR technologies have the potential to create immersive and interactive learning environments by overlaying digital information onto physical spaces. This can significantly enhance visitors' perceived learning outcomes.

For instance, a study by Ibáñez et colleagues (2014) found that AR applications in educational settings improved students' perceived learning effectiveness by making the learning process more engaging and interactive. Similarly, Han et al. (2019) reported that the use of AR in cultural heritage sites increased visitors' perceived learning by making historical information more accessible and engaging. These findings suggest that integrating AR and gamification can enhance the educational experience at cultural heritage sites, leading to higher overall satisfaction and a deeper appreciation for the cultural content.

Moreover, Bozzelli et colleagues (2019) importantly demonstrated that AR applications in museums helped visitors better understand and retain historical information by providing interactive and contextual overlays. The immersive nature of AR was shown to facilitate a more profound connection to the material, enhancing both short-term engagement and long-term retention. This is supported by Bacca et al. (2014), who conducted a comprehensive review of AR in educational settings and concluded that AR significantly improves learning performance and student motivation.

The enhanced learning outcomes facilitated by AR and gamification not only lead to educational benefits but also significantly impact life satisfaction. Learning outcomes, especially those achieved through engaging and interactive methods, are linked to various dimensions of wellbeing and life satisfaction. Theories of wellbeing, such as Seligman's PERMA model, emphasize the importance of engagement, meaning, and accomplishment, three elements closely related to effective learning outcomes (Seligman, 2011). When visitors to cultural heritage sites engage deeply with the content through AR and gamification, they not only gain knowledge but also experience a sense of accomplishment and purpose, significantly boosting their life satisfaction.

Research has shown that learning experiences that are immersive and interactive, such as those provided by AR, can enhance cognitive and emotional engagement (Huang & Soman, 2013). This heightened engagement can lead to more profound learning outcomes, which in turn contribute to a greater sense of achievement and fulfilment. The concept of lifelong learning, associated with higher levels of personal development and wellbeing, supports the relationship between continuous learning opportunities facilitated by AR and increased life satisfaction (Boeren, 2016).

Moreover, the use of gamification elements in educational contexts has been shown to enhance motivation and engagement, leading to better learning outcomes (Alsawaier, 2018; Li et al., 2023). When these gamified learning experiences are applied in cultural heritage sites, they not only make the visits more enjoyable but also contribute to the visitors' sense of achievement and purpose. Achieving meaningful goals, a key predictor of life satisfaction, is thus promoted through these interactive experiences (Diener et al., 2018).

Another critical aspect is the social dimension of learning. Collaborative learning environments, supported by AR and gamification, foster social interactions and collective problem-solving skills (Cheng & Tsai, 2013). These social interactions can enhance life satisfaction by fulfilling the human need for connection and community.

Shared learning experiences at cultural heritage sites can therefore contribute to both individual and collective wellbeing.

Thus, based on the previous literature and the above discussions, the following hypotheses are proposed:

Hypothesis

> **H1.** PEOU of AR technology positively influences the enjoyment derived from the gamification experience.
> **H2.** PU of AR technology positively influences the enjoyment derived from the gamification experience.
> **H3.** The enjoyment derived from the gamification experience positively impacts the level of visitor engagement.
> **H4.** The level of visitor engagement positively impacts the perceived learning effect.

H5. The perceived learning effects positively impact visitors' life satisfaction.

The proposed conceptual framework is shown in Figure 5.1.

5.3   Materials and Method

5.3.1   Sample and Materials

Participants were recruited through Prolific. A total of 164 participants completed the survey, which was deemed adequate for Structural Equation Modeling analyses, as per the guidelines suggested by Kline (2015).

Data quality checks for missing values, distribution anomalies, and outliers were performed using SPSS (version 26), revealing no significant issues.

To mitigate social desirability bias and common method variance (Podsakoff et al., 2003), the anonymity and confidentiality of participants were strongly emphasized, and participation was both voluntary and uncompensated. The survey design also separated questions for independent and dependent variables to minimize bias.

Descriptive statistics, reliability analyses, and evaluations of demographics and construct internal consistency were conducted using SPSS. For Partial Least Squares analysis, SmartPLS 3.0 was utilized to assess the study model. The analysis followed the standard two-step SEM approach, examining both the measurement model (for validity and reliability) and the structural model. The bootstrapping method with 5000 resamples was employed to determine the significance of path coefficients and loadings (Hair et al., 2019).

The sample consisted of 39% female (n = 64) and 61% male (n = 100) participants. Regarding educational background, 53.7% (n = 88) had a bachelor's degree, 26.8% (n = 44) had a high school diploma, and 19.5% (n = 32) held a master's degree. Geographically, the participants were primarily from Europe (66.5%, n = 109), followed by North America (11%, n = 18), Australia (9.8%, n = 16), South America (6.7%, n = 11), and Asia (6.1%, n = 10). In terms of experience with AR, 53% (n = 87) identified as beginners, 37.8% (n = 62) as intermediates, 6.1% (n = 10) as advanced users, 2.4% (n = 4) had no experience, and 0.6% (n = 1)

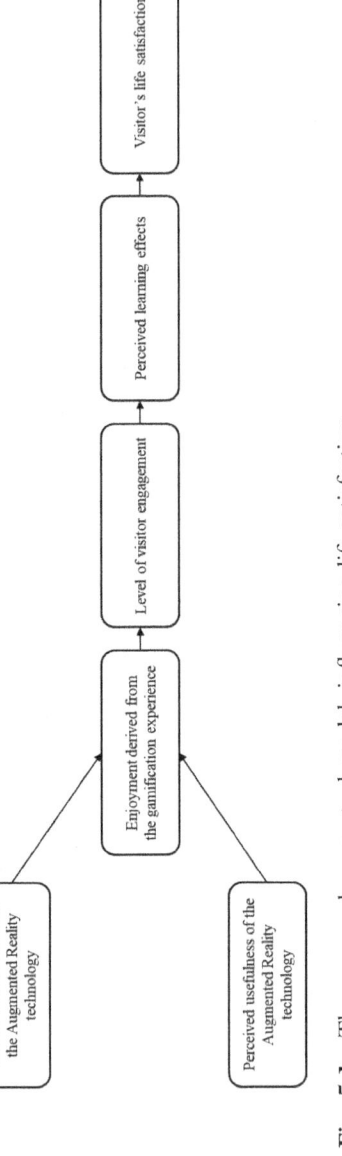

Fig. 5.1   The proposed conceptual model: influencing life satisfaction

were experts. The respondents' ages ranged from 19 to 66 years, with a mean age of 29.80 (SD = 8.38).

5.3.2 Questionnaire

To test the proposed hypotheses, a comprehensive survey instrument was designed utilizing established constructs from the literature. Participants were asked to rate their agreement with each statement using a 7-point Likert scale ranging from 1 ("Totally disagree") to 7 ("Totally agree").

In the initial section of the survey, participants were presented with a scenario set in an ancient Roman amphitheatre. They were asked to imagine being part of an AR journey that included various gamification elements such as avatar selection, quest storytelling, artifact collection, and rewards.

PEOU and PU of the AR technology were measured using scales adapted from Davis (1989). PEOU was assessed with a 3-item scale including items like "The AR experience would be understandable and clear" and "Using the AR headset would require minimal effort" (α = .81). PU was measured using a 5-item scale, including items such as "The AR tour would enhance the effectiveness of the tasks I have in mind" and "The AR tour would make it easier to accomplish the tasks I have in mind" (α = .94).

Enjoyment derived from the gamification experience was measured using a 5-item scale from Eppmann et al. (2018), including statements such as "Playing the game would be fun" and "My gaming experience would be pleasurable" (α = .91).

The level of visitor engagement was measured using a 3-item scale adapted from Seligman (2011), with items like "I would be absorbed and engaged while doing the AR tour" and "I would find myself 'in the zone' during the AR tour" (α = .66).

The perceived learning effect was measured using a scale from Baydas and Cicek (2019), with items including "I would learn about the history of the Roman amphitheatre during the AR tour" and "The AR tour would help me achieve my learning goals" (α = .88).

Life satisfaction was measured using a 4-item scale from Larsen and Diener (1985), including statements such as "I would be satisfied with my life thanks to experiences with AR visiting cultural heritage sites" and "I would achieve important personal goals through using AR for visiting cultural heritage sites" (α = .89).

Basic socio-demographic information was also collected, including gender, age, education, job occupation, and AR experience.

5.4   Results

5.4.1   Measurement Model

Initially, the convergent validity of the model was assessed by examining factor loadings, CR, and AVE. For the model to be considered valid, the values need to exceed specific thresholds: factor loadings should be above 0.5, CR should exceed 0.7, and AVE should be greater than 0.5 (Hair et al., 2009; 2019).

The results, summarized in Table 5.1, indicate that all measured values surpassed these recommended thresholds. Factor loadings for each construct item were above the 0.5 benchmark, confirming that each item significantly contributed to its corresponding construct. CR values were all above 0.7, indicating that the constructs were reliably measured by their respective items. Finally, AVE values exceeded 0.5, demonstrating that more than half of the variance of each construct was captured by its indicators, supporting the convergent validity of the model.

Furthermore, these findings suggest a robust measurement model where the constructs are well-represented by their indicators, ensuring that the model's validity holds for further analysis. The adherence to these thresholds is critical as it confirms that the constructs measured are both consistent and reliable, providing a solid foundation for evaluating the structural relationships within the model (Fornell & Larcker, 1981).

Subsequently, we evaluated the discriminant validity of the model using the HTMT ratio of correlations, which is derived from the multitrait-multimethod matrix. This approach helps to ascertain that each construct is distinct from the others, ensuring that they are not only measuring different phenomena but also doing so accurately.

As for the HTMT ratio, according to Kline (2015), a value below 0.85 indicates satisfactory discriminant validity. In our analysis, all the HTMT values were below this threshold, confirming that the constructs in our model are sufficiently distinct from one another. This finding aligns with the recommendations of Henseler et al. (2015), who advocated for the use of HTMT as a more reliable criterion for assessing discriminant validity compared to traditional methods such as the Fornell-Larcker criterion (Table 5.2).

Table 5.1 Convergent validity

Construct	Indicator	Item	Loading	Alpha	CR	AVE
PEOU	PEOU1	It's easy to use the AR headset.	.719***	.812	.887	.723
	PEOU2	The AR experience could be understandable and clear.	.904***			
	PEOU3	Using the AR headset could require minimum effort.	.672***			
PU	PU1	By going on the AR tour, I will improve my ability to accomplish the tasks I have in mind.	.852***	.943	.956	.813
	PU2	By going on the AR tour, I will save time for the tasks I have in mind.	.812***			
	PU3	By going on the AR tour, I will enhance the effectiveness of the tasks I have in mind.	.899***			
	PU4	The AR tour will make it easier to accomplish the tasks I have in mind.	.913***			
	PU5	The AR Tour will be useful in accomplishing the tasks I have in mind.	.901***			
ENJOY	ENJOY1	Playing the game would be fun.	.850***	.911	.934	.741
	ENJOY2	I would like to play the game.	.825***			
	ENJOY3	My gaming experience would be pleasurable.	.876***			
	ENJOY4	I think playing the game would be very entertaining.	.892***			
	ENJOY5	I would play this game for its own sake, not only when being asked to.	.663***			

(continued)

Table 5.1   (continued)

Construct	Indicator	Item	Loading	Alpha	CR	AVE
ENGAG	ENGAG1	I would just be absorbed and engaged while doing the AR tour.	.582***	.658	.793	.580
	ENGAG2	Time would pass so fast while doing the AR tour.	.632***			
	ENGAG3	I would find myself "in the zone" while doing the AR tour.	.924***			
PERLEAR	PERLEAR1	I would learn about the history of the Roman amphitheatre during the AR tour.	.741***	.878	.911	.672
	PERLEAR2	It would contribute to my learning while getting immediate feedback for every question I might have during the AR tour	.756***			
	PERLEAR3	Doing the AR tour would help me achieve the learning goals.	.824***			
	PERLEAR4	I feel that I would make an effort to learn during the AR tour.	.726***			
	PERLEAR5	I would feel more positive towards topics regarding the Roman amphitheatre while doing the AR tour.	.795***			
LIFESAT	LIFESAT1	My living conditions would feel excellent when using AR for visiting cultural heritage sites	.814***	.893	.925	.756
	LIFESAT2	I would be satisfied with my life thanks to experiences with AR visiting cultural heritage sites	.801***			

(continued)

Table 5.1 (continued)

Construct	Indicator	Item	Loading	Alpha	CR	AVE
	LIFESAT3	I would achieve important personal goals through using AR for visiting cultural heritage sites	.798***			
	LIFESAT4	The use of AR in visiting cultural heritage sites would contribute to my happiness	.871***			

Notes ***All standardized factor loadings are significant at the 0.01% level

Table 5.2 Discriminant validity

	ENGAG	PERLEAR	PEOU	PU	LIFESAT	ENJOY
ENGAG						
PERLEAR	.687					
PEOU	.399	.594				
PU	.435	.572	.431			
LIFESAT	.636	.750	.614	.558		
ENJOY	.727	.778	.566	.535	.780	

5.4.2 Structural Model

In this study, we employed a resampling technique with 5,000 samples, following the methodology suggested by Hair et al. (2009), to rigorously assess the structural model. This robust approach allows for a thorough evaluation of the hypothesized relationships within the model.

Thus, based on our statistical analysis, the results indicate that PEOU of AR technology has a significant positive impact on the enjoyment derived from the gamification experience ($\beta = 0.370$; t-value = 5.331; p < 0.01), thereby supporting our first hypothesis. Similarly, PU of AR technology also positively and significantly influences the enjoyment derived from the gamification experience ($\beta = 0.360$; t-value = 5.881; p < 0.01), confirming our second hypothesis.

Furthermore, the enjoyment derived from the gamification experience significantly enhances the visitor's engagement level ($\beta = 0.637$; t-value =

13.224; p < 0.001), thereby supporting our third hypothesis. This finding aligns with existing literature suggesting that enjoyment is a critical driver of user engagement in gamified environments (Koivisto & Hamari, 2019; Sailer et al., 2017).

Moreover, the visitor's engagement level significantly impacts the perceived learning effects ($\beta = 0.622$; t-value $= 13.732$; $p < 0.001$), thus supporting our fourth hypothesis. This result is consistent with studies indicating that higher engagement levels lead to better learning outcomes (Huang & Soman, 2013; Ibáñez et al., 2020).

Lastly, the perceived learning effect significantly influences the visitor's life satisfaction ($\beta = 0.672$; t-value $= 16.262$; $p < 0.001$), thereby supporting our final hypothesis. This finding is corroborated by research highlighting the link between effective learning experiences and overall life satisfaction (Diener et al., 2018; Seligman, 2011).

The explanatory power of the model is demonstrated by the variance explained (R^2 values) in the key constructs. PEOU and PU of AR technology together accounted for 36.9% of the variance in the enjoyment derived from the gamification experience.

The enjoyment derived from the gamification experience explained 40.6% of the variance in the visitor's engagement level. The visitor's engagement level accounted for 38.7% of the variance in the perceived learning effect, while the perceived learning effect explained 45.2% of the variance in life satisfaction.

These R^2 values indicate a substantial explanatory power of the model, underscoring the significant role of AR technology and gamification in enhancing visitor experiences and overall satisfaction (Table 5.3).

Table 5.3 Structural model

Hypothesis	Description	Beta	t-value	Decision
H1	PEOU → ENJOY	.370***	5.331	Supported
H2	PU → ENJOY	.360***	5.881	Supported
H3	ENJOY → ENGAG	.637***	13.224	Supported
H4	ENGAG → PERLEAR	.622***	13.732	Supported
H5	PERLEAR → LIFESAT	.672***	16.262	Supported

5.5   General Discussion and Conclusions

Recent studies have underscored the significance of integrating AR and gamification into educational and other practical contexts, illuminating their potential to boost engagement and learning outcomes. Notably, Lampropoulos and Kinshuk (2024) have called for further research into the synergies between AR and gamification, particularly in educational settings, to understand their combined effects on learning and user satisfaction. Similarly, Weng et al. (2023) emphasized the need for exploring the long-term impacts of these technologies on users. These calls for research signal a growing interest in how these technologies can be leveraged to enhance user experiences and outcomes.

Building on this reasoning and our results, the integration of AR and gamification into cultural heritage site experiences offers significant implications for both theoretical advancements and practical applications. Theoretically, this integration extends TAM, originally developed by Davis (1989), which posits that PU and PEOU are critical determinants of technology adoption. Research corroborating this model, such as findings from Cheng et al. (2023) and Marasco et al. (2018), demonstrates that PU and PEOU of AR significantly enhance the enjoyment derived from gamified experiences, a key factor in technology acceptance (Tussyadiah, 2018).

This enhanced enjoyment, a product of the seamless integration of gamification elements with AR applications, emerges as a primary driver of visitor engagement at cultural heritage sites. Supporting this, Seligman (2011) asserts that enjoyable activities significantly contribute to well-being, which is echoed by studies like those of Koivisto and Hamari (2019) and Sailer et al. (2017) that illustrate the motivational power of gamification in boosting user engagement. The results from these studies suggest that the combined use of AR and gamification not only creates engaging experiences but also enriches visitor interactions at these sites.

Furthering this line of inquiry, our study links the level of visitor engagement to perceived learning outcomes, reinforcing the notion that higher engagement leads to better educational experiences (Huang & Soman, 2013; Ibáñez et al., 2020). Additionally, the positive relationship between perceived learning effects and life satisfaction supports wellbeing theories that emphasize the importance of engaging in meaningful and fulfilling activities (Seligman, 2011; Diener et al., 2018). This comprehensive model demonstrates that effective use of AR and gamification can enhance not only the educational value of cultural heritage sites but also contribute to visitors' overall life satisfaction, proving that these technologies have substantial practical implications beyond their theoretical benefits.

From a practical perspective, the findings offer valuable insights for cultural heritage managers and technology developers. The study underscores the importance of designing AR applications that are both user-friendly and useful. Ensuring that these applications are easy to navigate and provide valuable content can significantly enhance visitor enjoyment and engagement. For instance, integrating intuitive interfaces and relevant, engaging content can cater to tech-savvy younger audiences who are accustomed to digital experiences.

Additionally, incorporating gamification elements such as rewards, challenges, and interactive storytelling can transform passive visits into active and enjoyable experiences. These elements can increase visitor satisfaction and encourage repeat visits, fostering long-term engagement and loyalty. Furthermore, gamified AR experiences can facilitate social interactions among visitors, enhancing the overall visitor experience through collaborative enjoyment and shared discovery.

While this study provides a framework for understanding the impact of AR and gamification on visitor experiences, several avenues for future research remain. First, further studies could explore the long-term effects of AR and gamified experiences on visitor learning and life satisfaction. Longitudinal studies would provide deeper insights into how these experiences influence visitors over time.

Second, future research could examine the specific elements of gamification that are most effective in enhancing engagement and learning outcomes. Understanding which game-design elements (e.g., points, leaderboards, badges) are most impactful can help refine AR applications for maximum benefit.

Lastly, exploring the potential negative effects of AR and gamification, such as over-reliance on technology or reduced appreciation of physical heritage sites, would provide a more balanced view of these technologies' impact.

Case Study Insights Box. Travel Verse: Transforming Travel with AI and VR for an Immersive Experience

Travel Verse is an innovative startup founded in early 2023 by Federico Lima and Ivan Allevi. The company specializes in revolutionizing the travel industry through the integration of artificial intelligence (AI) and virtual reality (VR) technologies. This visionary approach aims to provide an immersive and interactive travel experience, making destinations more attractive and accessible to potential travellers.

The inception of Travel Verse was inspired by a vision during a trip to Dubai.

Upon returning to Italy, Federico and Ivan established the company to address the challenges faced by the tourism sector, particularly in tour operations and hospitality services. Travel Verse's mission is to enhance the travel experience and streamline operations through technological innovation. The company's vision is to be at the forefront of travel tech, continuously pushing the boundaries of what is possible in the travel industry.

Travel Verse offers a unique value proposition through its AI-powered **Generative Engine** and **Virtual Concierge** service. These technologies address high operational costs, staff shortages, and the increasing demand for instant service and information.

The **Virtual Concierge**, built on a proprietary MIBO architecture, provides guests with detailed information and services autonomously, accessible via smart devices throughout the hotel.

The integration of advanced technologies at Travel Verse significantly contributes to individual and societal well-being. By creating **digital twins** of physical locations using 3D modelling, lidar technology, and VR/AR, Travel Verse offers travellers a virtual preview of their destinations, enhancing their planning and anticipation experiences. This not only enriches the travel experience but also promotes cultural heritage and education, especially through partnerships with platforms like Fortnite, where users can explore historic sites interactively.

Moreover, the virtual concierge improves operational efficiency in hotels, ensuring guests receive timely and personalized services, thereby increasing overall satisfaction. For tour operators and travel agencies, the immersive virtual environments facilitate better decision-making and customized travel planning, making the process more engaging and informative.

In conclusion, Travel Verse's innovative approach harnesses the power of AI and VR to transform the travel industry. By offering immersive experiences and enhancing service delivery, the company plays a pivotal role in improving the well-being of travellers and contributing positively to the society at large.

Martina Marchese, *Project Manager*, Travel Verse

Case Study Insights Box. Agricolus: Making AgriTech Sustainable

Agricolus is an innovative SME that develops **digital tools** for the **agricultural sector**. Founded in 2017 in Perugia, Umbria—the "green heart" of Italy—the company supports the work of the main actors of the agrifood chain.

"**Multidisciplinary**" is the adjective that distinguishes Agricolus team: **Agronomists** working closely with **developers**, **data analysts** and **GIS technicians**, **communication** and **marketing coordinators**, **administrative** and **finance personnel**.

The peculiarity is to have an internal **Research and Development** area able to independently process data from satellite, develop forecast models and new features that meet the demands of the market and the needs of farmers. The idea to create Agricolus was born from the passion of the co-founders for the Umbrian territory, especially for the agricultural fields and the role of farmers. Hence the intuition to spread the use of the innovative technologies for agriculture in Italy, in order to help the sector struggling with climate change and other challenges to better monitor crops and improve the agronomic management.

Agricolus platform has been developed to meet this need. It is composed of the main applications of **precision agriculture**: From geolocated field mapping to satellite imagery with vegetation indices, forecast models for phenology, irrigation, fertilization, pest and diseases, prescription maps for fertilization, sustainability indicators, and other features. The value is having all these tools available within a single, easy-to-use platform, able to integrate data and provide farmers with a **Decision Support System** (DSS), in order to act in the right time according to the real health conditions of the crop.

According to a study published by FAO (Food and Agriculture Organisation of the United Nations), the world population will increase by more than a third by 2050: This means that we will need 60% more food than is available today. How can farmers produce more with the same area of arable land (not to mention climate change and the consequent risk of pests and diseases) and with resources that are becoming increasingly limited? The innovative technologies are driving a process called "sustainable intensification": The increase of productivity goes at the same pace as the reduction of inputs used—water, fertilisers, plant protection products - in favour of the environmental and economic sustainability of agricultural production.

AgriTech tools are therefore necessary to collect, interpret and store information in order to make data-driven decisions. By using them farmers can improve yield quality by reducing the use of inputs (water, treatments, fertilizers) up to 20%, and make the activities in the field more effective.

Valeria Morè, *Communication Manager*, Agricolus s.r.l.

CHAPTER 6

Sustainable Digital Business Models as Facilitators for Individual and Societal Wellbeing. A Qualitative Case Study of a Digital Platform for Seamless Healthcare Service Access

Abstract The digital transformation has led to the development of Sustainable Digital Business Models (SDBMs), which prioritize environmental and social impacts. In industries like healthcare, coordinating stakeholder relationships is a challenge, often resulting in a "sustainable" oriented DBM. Despite the growing importance of SDBMs in healthcare, research on value generation, delivery, and capture for stakeholders remains limited. This chapter, by using a qualitative research design, explores Pyllola, an Italian startup offering telemedicine consultations and prescription services. Pyllola facilitates access to medical care by leveraging digital technologies, improving efficiency for both Italian citizens and foreigners in Italy. The findings highlight the significance of Pyllola's SDBM in value creation, delivery, and capture, emphasizing its positive impact on individual and societal wellbeing. Additionally, the study discusses the importance of sustainability in digital business models and its theoretical and managerial implications.

Keywords Digital technologies · Digitalization · Digital business models · Sustainable digital business models · Healthcare · Value

103

A. Sestino and L. Nasta, *The Digital Paradigm Shift for a New Business DNA*, https://doi.org/10.1007/978-3-031-76238-3_6

creation · Value capture · Value delivery · Accessibility · Sustainable purpose

6.1   Introduction and Overview of the Study

The advent of digitalization has exerted a profound and transformative influence upon the healthcare sector, crafting a new paradigm shift characterized by the emergence of novel practices, technological products, and services (Gjellebæk et al., 2020; Menvielle et al., 2017).

The digital transformation has profoundly reshaped the landscape of the healthcare sector, catalysing a paradigm shift in service delivery and business models (Sestino et al., 2024). Such a pervasive digital transformation has not only facilitated the integration of innovative medical technologies but has also engendered the development of entirely new Digital Business Models within the healthcare domain (Bresciani et al., 2021b; León et al., 2016). The new digital tools have facilitated seamless communication between healthcare providers and patients, reducing barriers to access and improving patient engagement (Oldenburg et al., 2020; Tanniru, 2019), contributing to the diffusion of new value (Balta et al., 2021).

Furthermore, the adoption of data-driven approaches has empowered healthcare organizations to make informed decisions, optimize resource allocation, and personalize treatment plans (Topol, 2019). Importantly, the digital transformation has spurred the evolution of traditional healthcare business models into digitally driven models, characterized by a focus on data-driven insights, interoperability, and patient-centred care (Lu, 2020). As a result, healthcare providers are increasingly embracing a holistic, interconnected approach, leveraging digital technologies to enhance not only clinical outcomes but also the overall patient experience.

6.2   Digital Business Models
and Sustainable Digital Business Models

Digital Business Models in healthcare inherently possess the qualities of sustainability due to their primary focus on patient-centric actions (Oderanti et al., 2021). The fundamental purpose of these models is rooted in enhancing patient care, accessibility, and overall healthcare outcomes.

Indeed, by leveraging digital technologies, such as telemedicine, electronic health records, and remote monitoring, these models aim to streamline healthcare processes, reduce inefficiencies, and ultimately improve the quality of patient experiences (Faggini et al., 2021).

When including a "digital perspective", literature suggests that sustainable digital business model (hereafter SDBM) refers to an approach wherein an organization leverages digital technologies to generate value while simultaneously minimizing negative environmental, ethical, and social impacts (Barth et al., 2021; Bocken et al., 2014; Menvielle et al., 2017; Schaltegger & Burritt, 2018). Such an approach entails the integration of socially responsible practices into the core operations of a digital business, ensuring long-term viability.

Based on seminal research (Bocken et al., 2014; Schaltegger & Burritt, 2018) the concept of sustainable digital business model is deeply oriented in integrating environmental, social, and economic dimensions into the core framework of business operations (Del Giudice et al., 2022). A sustainable business model seeks to create value not only for shareholders but also for broader stakeholders, encompassing the wellbeing of the environment and society, and thus, by nature the healthcare domain may be particularly interesting because of its intrinsic nature. The healthcare sector plays a pivotal role in promoting public health and wellbeing through the delivery of medical services, preventive measures, and therapeutic interventions (Pronk et al., 2021), and its intrinsic and complex nature arises from the intersection of medical science, technological advancements, regulatory frameworks, and socio-economic factors, necessitating a comprehensive understanding for effective policy formulation and healthcare management (Jones & Brown, 2018).

Thus, the digital paradigm shift into sustainable business model, facilitated by new digital technologies (Bocken et al., 2014; Schaltegger & Burritt, 2018), may be particularly effective in sustaining healthcare, by emphasizing long-term resilience, ethical practices, and a holistic approach to corporate success, making sustainable business models a strategic tool for fostering enduring prosperity while addressing global challenges as in the healthcare (Shilpa & Kaur, 2022). Such an emphasis on patient-oriented initiatives not only aligns with ethical imperatives but also contributes to the long-term viability of the healthcare ecosystem (Faggini et al., 2021; Schiavone et al., 2021). Thus, through the integration of innovative technologies and patient-centric approaches, Digital Business Models in healthcare demonstrate a commitment to sustainable practices, ensuring a lasting positive impact on both individual wellbeing and the broader healthcare landscape.

Importantly, the imperative to ensure access to medical care for patients, irrespective of the prevailing healthcare system and geographic location, is fundamentally rooted in the inherent right to health and deep digital-oriented perspective may sustain such efforts (Sahoo et al., 2023). Inherent in the principles of healthcare equity and human dignity is the conviction that individuals should have unfettered access to essential medical services, even when abroad (Haynes, 2003; Foglia et al., 2024; Sahoo et al., 2023). For instance, telemedicine services may enhance social and environmental domains (Foglia et al., 2024), make accessible several services independently from the geographical locations, overcoming the traditional barriers improving the access to care (Barbosa et al., 2021).

Technological advancements present a unique opportunity to transcend traditional healthcare paradigms, fostering the development of sustainable business models that are inherently technology driven. Through leveraging such innovations, it becomes conceivable to establish frameworks dedicated to creating and disseminating new value by safeguarding access to fundamental healthcare services, irrespective of the geographical constraints that have historically posed challenges to universal medical care provision.

Based on the premises above, this paper seeks to enhance the growing body of literature on sustainable Digital Business Models in healthcare (Léon et al., 2016; Hwang and Christensen, 2008; Oderanti et al., 2021). Our contribution aims to present an extensive, intricate, and stakeholder-centric perspective on the mechanisms governing value creation, delivery, and capture within the complex business ecosystem of sustainable digital healthcare models. This approach aligns with the sustainable digital business model concept (Bocken et al., 2014; Schaltegger & Burritt, 2018).

The formal objective of this research is to comprehend how value is generated, disseminated, and appropriated for diverse stakeholders in digital platforms ensuring global access to healthcare. To address this inquiry, we employed the qualitative research method of a case study (Yin, 2017), focusing on the case of Pyllola, an Italian digital startup providing a platform for video consultations with online doctors, also facilitating medical assistance through prescriptions or advice, allows users to request medication refills with a dematerialized prescription in case of loss, and addresses common health conditions with known and easily prescribable treatments, independently of their geographical location and, importantly, independently of the national healthcare service of their country of origin. Thus, in this last explorative chapter, through a qualitative research design (Goia et al., 2013), we analysed data related to the case study Pyllola (Yin et al., 2013). The data collection involved both primary and secondary sources, including online documentation, archival documents, in-depth interviews, and focus group sessions with company management and stakeholders.

6.3   Materials and Methods

6.3.1   Research Design and Pyllola as a Research Setting

Through the utilization of an exploratory research design, a qualitative methodology has been implemented to comprehensively analyse an exceptionally relevant case study (Meredith, 1998; Yin, 2017). As suggested by Yin (2013; 2017), such a methodological approach based on the analysis of single case study could entail an *in-depth* examination of a singular case or specific instance to garner comprehensive and hidden insights. In addressing the distinctive nature of the case and the absence of an established theoretical framework, a structured exploratory case-based study design was implemented, drawing inspiration from the works of Meredith (1998) and Yin (2013; 2017).

Thus, coherently with the goal of this paper, this research methodology is particularly apt when addressing complex and contextual "how" or "why" research questions. The selected case in this paper is Pyllola, which constitutes an optimal solution for travellers, both Italian and foreign, who find themselves outside their home country and require a resupply of prescription medications or a medical consultation. On the basis of the peculiarities of this novel business model, the proposed methodology and the research structure is deemed appropriate when researchers refrain from formulating pre-emptive propositions and hypotheses, as outlined by Mills et colleagues (2010), in the attempt to thoroughly explore the case, employing diverse data sources such as interviews, documents, and observations to achieve a holistic understanding of the examined phenomenon (Yin, 2013; 2017). Pyllola.com is an Italy-based company, operated by Pyllola s.r.l., in Rome, Italy.

According to the official website of this digital platform (Pyllola Website: https://it.pyllola.com) all their physicians and medical doctors are fully licensed in Italy, comprising both family doctors and general practitioners, proficient in both English and Italian, with some possessing proficiency in additional languages. Importantly, also by considering the topicalities of the Italian healthcare sector (Parente et al., 2018), Pyllola may be an interesting case study since its goals are also directed to both enhance the patients' journey through the provision of convenient, cost-efficient, and dependable services, and importantly, because the platform extends such services to travellers with limited access to healthcare services in foreign territories.

As aforementioned above, this research focus centred on an extreme case involving a sustainable digital business model located within a specific geographical area, as per the criteria set forth by Seawright and Gerring (2008). Indeed, the adoption of a digital business model facilitating prescription medication resupply and medical consultations for both local and foreign travellers outside their home region as Pyllola, could be considered sustainable, as it aligns with the principles of long-term value generation and balance among economic, social, and environmental benefits. According to literature, sustainable business models encompass social and environmental responsibility, ethical practices, and minimizing negative environmental impact (Bocken et al., 2014; Schaltegger & Burritt, 2018).

This approach ensures economic resilience and adaptability over time, contributing to a lasting and positive life cycle (Boons et al., 2013; Cillo et al., 2019; Geissdoerfer et al., 2016). Therefore, the integration of such a digital business model not only meets immediate healthcare needs but also addresses broader sustainability objectives.

6.3.2   Research Design and Data Analysis

On the basis of the seminal literature on this domain (Yin, 2013; 2017), in this paper we gathered and examined both primary and secondary data to investigate the Sustainable Digital Business Model, structured for consultation and medication prescription. Specifically, the mission was aimed to comprehend and investigate the design of such business model in coordinating the creation, delivery, and capture of value. To reach a correct data triangulation (Yin, 2017), we leveraged multiple sources of evidence, including online documentation (Phase 1), archival documents (Phase 2), in-depth interviews (Phase 3 and focus groups (Phase 4).

Phase 1. Online Documentation

The analysis was structured into four consecutive phases. Initially, in the first phase, the domain has been examined, specifically focusing on the Italian healthcare system to discern current trends, composition, and the availability of services offered by entities within the healthcare sector engaged in remote medical consultation and prescription services (e.g., as for medication prescription). Results of this analysis confirmed that the advent of digital telemedicine platforms has significantly altered interactions among various stakeholders in the Italian healthcare system. The traditional roles of state, regions, and enterprises have undergone transformation. Based on our preliminarily analysis, the state's involvement has shifted from exclusive regulation to collaborative decision-making with regional entities, introducing a multi-level governance approach. The healthcare system no longer solely dictates market access for medical devices or manages policies for specific healthcare services but, regional bodies, decision-makers, and health departments are now integral to the decision-making process (Schiavone). Regions now play a pivotal role in shaping access and policies, while enterprises navigate a complex landscape, requiring strategic alignment with both state and regional directives to effectively contribute to and navigate the evolving digital healthcare ecosystem, resulting in a multi-stakeholder ecosystem in where gaining a competitive advantage now entails strategic decision-making at regional and local levels on how to engage with these new entities and collaborate with diverse stakeholders.

The advent of telemedicine has brought substantial transformations to the Italian healthcare market. As highlighted by Wherton et colleagues (2022), telemedicine technologies have redefined patient-doctor interactions, fostered remote consultations, and enhanced accessibility by enabling newer digital business models. This shift has not only streamlined healthcare delivery but has also prompted a revaluation of traditional market dynamics, emphasizing the need for adaptability and strategic alignment with evolving technological landscapes (Baudier et al., 2021).

Phase 2. Archival Documents

In the second phase research also involved the screening of major articles from specialized press and official reports related to telemedicine and teleconsulting platforms. Subsequently, we gathered official archival documentation, such as websites, official social media publications, and data from digital platforms, mainly discussing Pyllola also by leveraging on platform specialized in online reviews allowing users to make informed decisions based on the experiences of other travellers (i.e., Tripadvisor), and social media platforms (i.e., Reddit as a social media platform and online community where users can submit content, participate in discussions, and vote on posts and comments).

Phase 3. In-Depth Interviews

In the third phase, by following Yin (2013; 2017) and Gill (2008), we employed interviews and focus groups as a part of our qualitative research method. Specifically, semi-structured interviews were conducted following the framework of the Business Model Canvas (Osterwalder & Pigneur, 2010), considering the objective of comprehending the Sustainable Digital Business Model. The interviews incorporated open-ended and free-response questions designed to gather opinions on the use and benefits of Pyllola, its underlying concept, and how the value proposition aimed to address issues of high social complexity. Additionally, targeted questions were posed to shed light on the consequences of adopting this platform in the realm of healthcare services. The interviews lasted approximately eighty minutes, and the findings were transcribed by researchers within the subsequent twenty-four hours.

Phase 4. Focus Group

Given the exploratory nature of the paper, the fourth phase involved conducting three distinct focus groups to investigate the value creation effects achieved by Pyllola through its sustainable business model. As suggested by seminal research focusing on the healthcare sector as well (i.e., Lamber & Loiselle, 2008), combining individual interviews and focus groups may be advantageous for researchers, generating complementary perspectives on the phenomenon for enrichment and confirmation of mutual findings. Notably, participants had no prior relationship with the researchers.

The focus groups have been organized with the ultimate goal of fostering discussions and eliciting nested insights (Kitzinger, 1995), particularly to illuminate the perceptions of stakeholders involved in different focus groups regarding the benefits arising from a business model like Pyllola's. The first focus group (FC1) involved healthcare practitioners directly engaged in medical consultations (physicians, $n = 8$), while the second (FC2) comprised entities within the healthcare system, including pharmaceutical operators (healthcare professionals, $n = 8$). Finally, the third focus group included potential consumers (consumers, $n = 10$). The focus groups were conducted remotely or at the premises of the Università Cattolica del Sacro Cuore in Rome, Interfaculty of Medicine, Surgery, and Economics, and the locations of LUISS Guido Carli in Rome, Italy.

Similar to the interviews, also these results have been transcribed verbatim immediately to facilitate subsequent analysis (Merriam & Tisdell, 2015). Then, to ensure rigour in qualitative data analysis, descriptive first-order terms (e.g., as for the quotations) and second-order themes (e.g., as for key emerging topics) were initially linked to the identified aggregate dimensions: (1) Actor operating as a Sustainable Digital Business Model in the healthcare system; (2) Boosters of relationships and interaction as part of the range of services offered in the private healthcare market; (3) Contribution to the co-creation of widespread value (consistent with business model sustainability).

Finally, to confirm and triangulate data and information collected from in-depth interviews and focus groups, additional sources have been explored too, such as those related to the secondary data from Pyllola's official website, specialized press, and other official reports (Phase 2). In analysing and interpreting the data, an inductive approach through thematic analysis was employed (Belk, 2017; Braun & Clarke, 2006).

6.4   FINDINGS

In accordance with the previously outlined methodology, this section examines how value is generated, delivered, and captured by various stakeholders through the proposed platform, with reference to the Digital Business Model (DBM). The findings highlight three main categories: (1) Pyllola as a facilitator of access to medical care; (2) Pyllola as a digital business model; and (3) Co-creation of value and its impact on individual and societal wellbeing.

6.4.1   Facilitator of Access to Medical Care

The Pyllola platform enables the reconfiguration of service portfolios for stakeholders within the ecosystem through a digital business model. By expanding their services, healthcare organizations (HOs) can provide comprehensive care to patients throughout their health journey. Specifically, Pyllola offers (1) Telemedicine Services, including (a) *Video Consultations with Online Doctors*, since Pyllola facilitates scheduling telemedicine appointments via video calls with qualified doctors; and (b) *Remote Medical Assistance*, since Pyllola ensures remote medical assistance, allowing patients to receive prescriptions or useful advice from healthcare professionals. Moreover, Pyllola also offers (2) Pharmacy Services, including (c) *Medication* Requests, since Pyllola enables users to request medication prescriptions through a digital prescription; and (d) *Management of Regular Medications:* Pyllola aids in managing regularly prescribed medications, providing a timely solution in case of loss or depletion without the need for a medical consultation.

Pyllola's business model centres on an online platform through which the company delivers digital healthcare services, such as teleconsultations and prescription renewals, leveraging a digital and dematerialized delivery method. Supported by a network of doctors and healthcare professionals, Pyllola aims to facilitate access to medical services and care that would otherwise be more expensive for tourists visiting Italy.

A healthcare professional (general practitioner, 36 y.o., M) confirmed that "Pyllola addresses the gaps that the National Health Service (NHS) cannot meet, especially for those who need quick and timely responses, such as tourists who might have difficulty accessing hospital services".

Similarly, the CEO of Pyllola stated, "The business model of Pyllola revolves around an online platform through which the company offers the provision of digital healthcare services, such as teleconsultation and pharmaceutical prescription renewal, using a digital and dematerialized delivery method. Thanks to a network of doctors and healthcare professionals licensed in Italy and participating in our initiative, the company's goal is to facilitate access to medical services and care that would otherwise be more costly for tourists visiting our country".

6.4.2 *Sustainable Digital Business Model: Impacts on Value Creation, Delivery, and Capture*

The business model adopted by Pyllola integrates various revenue streams, ensuring economic sustainability through competitive rates, advanced digital services, and a diverse range of offerings that provide convenience to users. This has solidified the company's position in the emerging landscape of online healthcare services. With direct access via smartphones and no additional apps or services to instal, Pyllola guarantees high accessibility, overcoming user reluctance towards installation practices.

Regarding the *Value Proposition* Pyllola's objective is to provide rapid and immediate assistance to patients nationwide, particularly for tourists and foreigners, through teleconsultations and one-time pharmaceutical prescriptions. Thus, by focusing on the case study, (1) the *Creation of Value* is realized by improving access to medical care for patients visiting Italy or those unable to contact their primary care physicians; (2) the *Value Delivery* is conducted through partnerships with licensed medical professionals in Italy; and (3) finally, the *Value Capture* occurs via reimbursement through the platform and direct payment from clients. Specifically, Pyllola charges a base fee of €89 for teleconsultation services and €49 for pharmaceutical prescriptions. This model operates as a business-to-consumer framework, targeting tourists directly without the need to rely on local healthcare facilities.

Therefore, the DBM embodied by the Pyllola platform involves various actors, primarily general practitioners, who participate at different levels in the healthcare services provided to patients. By creating a digital network, Pyllola delivers value to end patients, not only by enhancing their wellbeing through the services offered but also by addressing the shortcomings of the national healthcare system, making healthcare access homogeneous and equitably available. Consequently, the DBM contributes to the wellbeing of both individuals and the broader society in which it operates.

As noted in Focus Group 2, "Pyllola is extremely relevant as this digital solution can network doctors and patients, providing homogeneous services and allowing everyone to benefit from adequate healthcare services in case of emergency or inability to contact their primary care physician". This significance was also highlighted by Pyllola's legal officer, who stated, "The platform offers a highly competitive advantage to those who join the network, generating value for them as doctors and providing income for their services, but above all, for patients who can equitably access the offered services through digital channels.

This is particularly useful for tourists in Italy who, in the case of minor ailments or routine medication prescriptions, can avoid queues and waiting times at hospitals or medical offices by consulting our pool of doctors". The relevance of the DBM is further emphasized by Pyllola's CEO, who noted, "The segment we decided to focus on is that of tourists in Italy. Italy is one of the most sought-after destinations. However, during their stay, tourists may face difficulties accessing services, partly due to well-known language barriers".

6.4.3   *Value Co-Creation and Its Impact on Individual and Societal Wellbeing*

The Pyllola online platform is instrumental in co-creating value by offering specialized telemedicine services to tourists and foreigners in Italy, allowing them to access medical care in English. Through video consultations, electronic prescriptions, and facilitated access to medications, Pyllola enhances healthcare accessibility, reducing linguistic and logistical barriers. This not only promotes the individual wellbeing of travellers but also contributes to public health by ensuring more people receive timely and competent care.

Value co-creation through Pyllola occurs through active collaboration between patients and healthcare professionals. This telemedicine platform enables patients to take an active role in managing their health, with direct access to medical services in English. Patients can interact with doctors for diagnoses, consultations, and prescriptions more efficiently and transparently. Healthcare professionals, in turn, can offer personalized services and receive immediate feedback, improving the quality of care.

This synergy creates shared value benefiting both individuals and society, enhancing accessibility and the effectiveness of medical care. As recognized in Focus Group 1, "Indeed, by accessing the platform, the patient can be assured of having a sort of single access point for quick consultation and prescription of medications, stemming from the close collaboration between the doctor and the patient who proactively accesses the service". Additionally, as stated by a participant in Focus Group 2, "Pyllola aims to provide 'simple' and 'immediate' assistance through doctors capable of communicating in English (and other languages) via mobile phone or video call. The service does not require registration or any app installation. European and Italian legislation allows the use of electronic prescriptions, facilitating the completion of medical consultations when a prescription for basic or specific medications is needed".

The platform proposed by Pyllola represents an ideal solution for those seeking medical consultation without physically visiting hospitals, clinics, or medical facilities, as well as for foreign travellers needing prescription medications while away from home. Thus, Pyllola's primary objective is to ensure consistent healthcare support, always available online from any geographical location, as doctors are accessible online and can be "visited" and accessed virtually, i.e., through a video call.

Thus, Pyllola, as a Digital Business Model (DBM), exemplifies a compelling case study for examining the broad impacts of Digital Business Models on individual and societal wellbeing. By leveraging an online platform to deliver telemedicine services and electronic prescription management, Pyllola facilitates access to healthcare, particularly for tourists and foreigners in Italy who may face significant barriers in navigating the local healthcare system. This innovative approach addresses critical gaps left by traditional healthcare services, offering quick and efficient medical consultations and prescriptions, thereby enhancing the overall patient experience.

The platform's integration of digital tools ensures a seamless user experience, with direct access via smartphones and no need for additional apps, which increases accessibility and reduces user reluctance. Economically, Pyllola sustains itself through a diverse range of revenue streams, competitive pricing, and partnerships with licensed healthcare professionals, ensuring both the scalability and sustainability of the service. Moreover, by democratizing access to healthcare, Pyllola not only improves individual health outcomes but also contributes to public health by ensuring timely and competent care for a broader population.

The *co-creation* of value between patients and healthcare providers, facilitated by the platform, underscores the shared benefits of this model, enhancing the quality and efficiency of medical care through real-time feedback and personalized services. This synergy between technology and healthcare delivery highlights the potential of Digital Business Models to foster significant societal benefits, making healthcare more inclusive and equitable.

As such, Pyllola's model demonstrates how digital innovation may transform traditional sectors, providing a blueprint for other industries aiming to enhance service delivery and societal wellbeing through digital transformation.

6.4.4   The Relevance of the Sustainability "Component" in the Digital Business Model

Based on the findings above and based on the figure above (Fig. 6.1), Pyllola can be considered a *sustainable* digital business model due to its substantial positive impact on society, addressing both individual health needs and broader public health goals. Indeed, sustainability in this context is multifaceted, encompassing *economic viability*, *social inclusivity*, and *environmental* considerations (Bocken et al., 2014; Broccardo et al., 2023; Di Vaio, 2020; Schaltegger & Burritt, 2018).

Indeed, (1) *Economically*, Pyllola sustains itself through a well-integrated revenue model that includes competitive pricing for teleconsultations and electronic prescriptions. This financial structure ensures that the platform can continue to operate and expand without relying on unsustainable funding sources.

Moreover, (2) *Socially*, Pyllola promotes inclusivity by providing essential healthcare services to underserved populations, such as tourists and foreigners in Italy, who might otherwise struggle to access timely medical care due to language barriers and unfamiliarity with the local healthcare system.

By offering services in multiple languages and facilitating direct access via smartphones, Pyllola removes significant obstacles to healthcare access, contributing to the overall wellbeing of a diverse user base. This inclusive approach not only benefits individuals by providing them with immediate medical assistance but also enhances public health by reducing the burden on local healthcare facilities and ensuring that more people receive necessary care promptly.

Furthermore, (3) *Environmentally*, Pyllola's digital platform minimizes the need for physical infrastructure and travel, thereby reducing its carbon footprint. Patients can receive medical consultations and prescriptions online, which decreases the demand for in-person visits to healthcare facilities and the associated environmental costs, such as transportation emissions and resource use in medical offices.

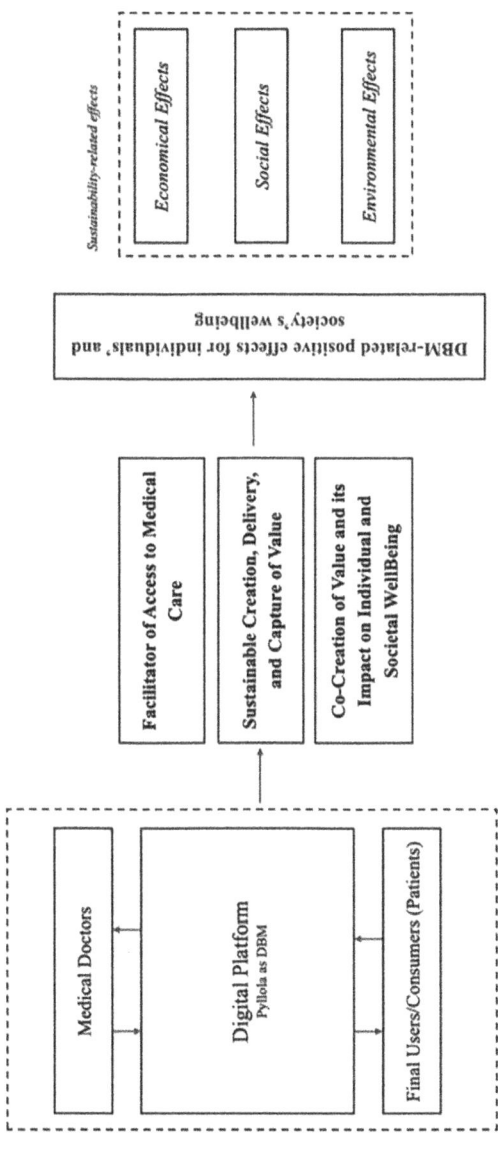

Fig. 6.1 Digital Business Model-related positive effects for individuals' and society's wellbeing

Moreover, Pyllola may foster a (4) *Collaborative ecosystem* among healthcare professionals, enabling a more efficient allocation of medical resources and expertise. This networked approach allows for the sharing of knowledge and best practices, improving the overall quality of care and supporting continuous professional development.

In essence, Pyllola may exemplify the concept of a sustainable digital business model since it integrates economic, social, and environmental sustainability. It demonstrates how digital innovation can meet current healthcare needs while promoting long-term societal benefits, making it a valuable case study for the broader implications of Digital Business Models in fostering sustainable development.

6.5   General Discussion and Conclusions

This study extends the current understanding of SDBM within the healthcare sector, emphasizing the transformative role of digital platforms like Pyllola in enhancing individual and societal wellbeing. Theoretically, this research bridges the gap identified in earlier studies regarding the generation, delivery, and capture of value through digital platforms in healthcare, as highlighted by Sestino et colleagues (2024) and Bresciani et colleagues (2021b). Our findings align with the assertions by Bocken et al. (2014) and Schaltegger and Burritt (2018), illustrating that digital business models can integrate environmental, social, and economic sustainability into their core operations effectively.

Through the detailed examination of Pyllola's operations, this study significantly enhances the discourse surrounding digital business models in healthcare. The platform exemplifies how digital innovations can transcend traditional barriers to healthcare access, providing timely and convenient services to a broader demographic. This case study aligns closely with the theories proposed by Oderanti et al. (2021), which emphasize the inherent sustainability of digital business models catalysed by their commitment to enhancing patient care and overall health outcomes.

Pyllola's approach, which leverages digital tools to facilitate real-time interactions between doctors and patients, demonstrates a practical application of these theories. The platform not only improves the efficiency of healthcare delivery but also ensures that these improvements are sustainable and beneficial on multiple fronts—social, economic, and environmental. By integrating value co-creation into its operations, Pyllola actively involves both service providers and users in a shared healthcare experience, thus enhancing the relevance and effectiveness of the medical advice and interventions provided.

Furthermore, this research underscores the role of sustainable practices within Pyllola's business model. The digital platform reduces the need for physical infrastructure, minimizes travel requirements for both patients and healthcare providers, and decreases the environmental footprint associated with traditional healthcare delivery methods. By doing so, Pyllola not only addresses immediate healthcare needs but also aligns with broader sustainability goals, such as reducing carbon emissions and promoting resource efficiency.

Practically, this research offers valuable insights for stakeholders in the healthcare industry, including policymakers, healthcare providers, and digital platform developers. By delineating how Pyllola enhances access to healthcare services through digital means, this study underscores the importance of supportive regulatory frameworks that facilitate the adoption of digital health solutions. For healthcare providers and entrepreneurs, the findings highlight the potential for digital platforms to expand their service reach and improve patient care, suggesting that investing in digital technologies can be a strategic move towards business sustainability and enhanced patient satisfaction.

The insights gained from Pyllola's model suggest that other healthcare providers could replicate or adapt these digital strategies to improve their service delivery, particularly in environments where access to medical care is challenging. Additionally, the model illustrates the potential for digital platforms to serve as a critical component in crisis response strategies, where immediate healthcare access is disrupted.

However, despite the findings, this study is not without limitations. The primary limitation stems from its focus on a single case study, which while providing in-depth insights, may limit the generalizability of the findings across different contexts or healthcare systems. The qualitative nature of the study, although rich in detailed understanding, might also overlook quantitative measures of impact and effectiveness that could further validate the findings. Additionally, the rapidly evolving nature of digital technologies and healthcare regulations may necessitate continuous updates to the study's conclusions to remain relevant.

CHAPTER 7

Overall Discussion, Trajectories and Conclusions: Towards a Holistic View of Digital Technologies Integrations for Individuals and Societal Wellbeing, and a New Business DNA

Abstract This chapter integrates findings from previous chapters, combining insights from a literature review and empirical studies with qualitative analysis. It explores the theoretical, managerial, marketing, and policymaking implications of emerging new digital technologies, emphasizing their role in redefining value propositions within firms aimed to enhance individuals' and societal wellbeing. Indeed, bearing in mind the objectives of the book outlined in the introductory chapter, as well as the need for a new approach to managing the Digital Paradigm Shift, one driven by a new business DNA increasingly oriented not only towards the satisfaction of needs but also towards the enhancement of individual wellbeing (as consumers, citizens, patients, tourists, etc.), and the welfare of the community and, society at large, we offer insights for future strategies in management, marketing, and policymaking.

Kewyords
Digital technologies
Digitalization
Digital business models
Consumers
Individuals

A. Sestino and L. Nasta, *The Digital Paradigm Shift for a New Business DNA*, https://doi.org/10.1007/978-3-031-76238-3_7

Societies
Sustainable development
Sustainability
Wellbeing
Management
Marketing

7.1   LINKING FIRMS' ORIGINAL PURPOSE, NEW DIGITAL TECHNOLOGIES, AND WELLBEING

7.1.1   *Affirming the New Holistic Perspective: Rediscovering Firms' Original Purpose and Its Linkage with New Technologies Exploitation*

In today's global landscape, the imperative of sustainability stands as a cornerstone of responsible business practices. At the heart of this ethos lies a commitment to addressing societal and environmental challenges, as outlined in the United Nations Sustainable Development Goals (SDGs).

Central to the concept of sustainability is not only mitigating environmental impact but also fostering inclusivity and meeting the needs of individuals and communities. Enterprises must therefore embrace a philosophy that not only recognizes their role in satisfying consumer demands but also acknowledges their responsibility to contribute positively to society. By anchoring themselves in this purpose-driven approach, firms can harness the transformative power of digital technologies. These innovations present unprecedented opportunities to reimagine and redesign their value propositions. By exploiting new digital technologies, as the ones examined in this book (e.g., IoT, AI, VR, and so on), managers and marketers can tailor their firms' offerings more precisely to consumer needs while promoting sustainability practices across their operations.

This "dual" focus not only enhances consumers' satisfaction, but importantly may also drive social impact by increasing individuals' wellbeing, life satisfaction, empowering local communities, and advancing equitable and seamless access to resources.

Furthermore, integrating digital solutions allows businesses to optimize resource allocation, reduce waste, and improve efficiency throughout their supply chains. By leveraging technology to monitor and manage environmental impacts, organizations can achieve tangible progress towards sustainability goals while maintaining competitiveness in a rapidly evolving marketplace.

In essence, the convergence of purpose-driven business strategies with digital innovation represents a powerful catalyst for positive change. It enables enterprises to forge a path towards sustainable growth, where economic success is intrinsically linked to societal wellbeing and environmental stewardship. By embracing this holistic approach, the firms of the future should not only "future-proof" their operations, but should also contribute meaningfully to a more equitable, resilient, and sustainable world.

7.1.2   A New "DNA" for Today's Firms

As explained above, and shown in this book, in the contemporary times, the role of firms is crucial as the integration of new technologies is not merely about incorporating tools but must be a holistic process and outcome capable of positively impacting not only business activities but also the wellbeing of individuals and society.

As emphasized in various discussions and literature offered in this book, the introduction of new technologies is not only essential for ensuring better working conditions through appropriate upskilling and reskilling, increasing work flexibility, promoting new conditions such as smart working, enhancing process efficiency, and providing significant support for human resources and managerial decision-making processes. Importantly, its main contribution is in restructuring firms' value proposition in the attempt to offer renewed products and services, with a greater (and renewed) market (and society) orientation.

Indeed, the focus of this book, however, shifts entirely to the contribution of new technologies in revitalizing the value propositions of firms, and on the variable affecting individuals' positive reactions to such technologies, when they perceive a possible greater wellbeing deriving from the utilization of such new technologies as a part of their journey.

This journey is not merely about the initial adoption of new technologies, but rather encompasses the entire spectrum of behavioural changes, learning curves, and adaptations required over time. It includes how individuals integrate these technologies into their daily lives and workplaces, modifying their routines and strategies to maximize the benefits offered by these innovations.

Moreover, the new journey is marked by a series of responses and adaptations, both psychological and practical. As individuals perceive improvements in their wellbeing, whether through enhanced efficiency, reduced stress, or greater life satisfaction, their journey reflects a positive feedback loop that encourages further exploration and acceptance of these technologies. This iterative process of adaptation and improvement is critical in understanding why and how new technologies are adopted and the sustained impact they can have on individual lives and society as a whole.

Thus, in the broader narrative of the book, this journey symbolizes not just the adoption of technology but a transformational path that leads to enhanced personal and professional wellbeing, aligning technological advances with human-centric benefits.

This reminds us that today's firms must combine the following three important pillars:

Pillar 1. The rediscovery of their original purpose, which is to meet individuals' (and societies') needs, driven by a conscious sustainable approach.

Pillar 2. The integration of new technologies to enhance their value propositions, offering better products and services by leveraging on innovative and sustainable business models.

Pillar 3. A greater focus on the final "recipients" of their efforts, the individuals as consumers, in a highly consumer-centric approach.

All this becomes an integral part of a new culture, a new "way to do", inspired by a renewed DNA of the firms. This transformation is not just about adopting new tools and technologies, but fostering a profound cultural shift within, and outside the organizations. It involves redefining the very essence of business operations and values, ensuring that technological integration aligns seamlessly with the broader mission of enhancing human and societal wellbeing (see Fig. 7.1).

In this new paradigm deriving by our proposed holistic approach, firms are driven by a purpose that transcends profit, focusing on sustainable and inclusive growth. This renewed DNA emphasizes an individual-centric approach, where the needs and wellbeing of individuals are at the forefront of business strategies. Thus, firms strive to create value through

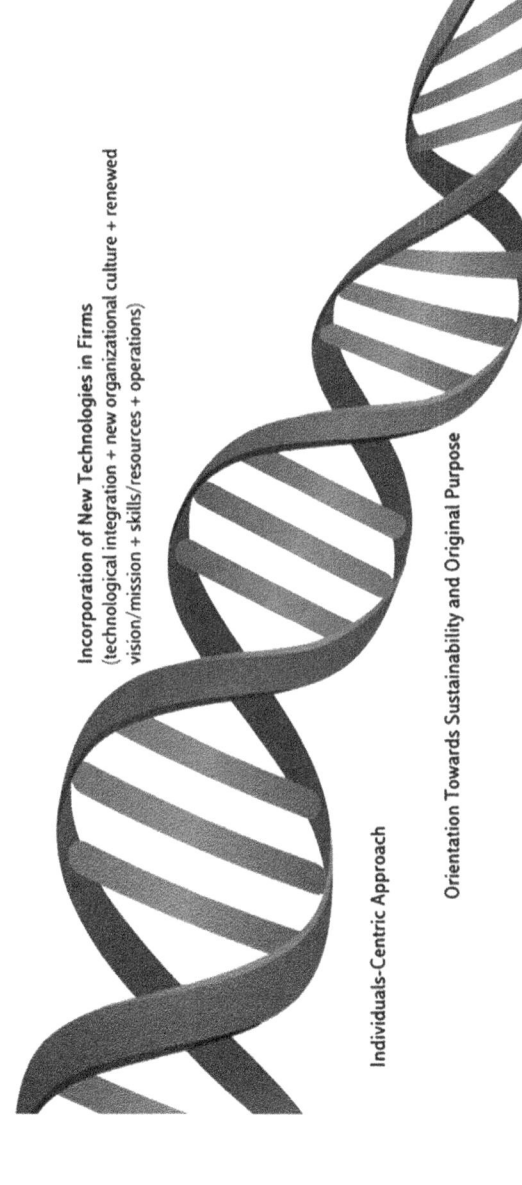

Incorporation of New Technologies in Firms
(technological integration + new organizational culture + renewed vision/mission + skills/resources + operations)

Orientation Towards Sustainability and Original Purpose

Individuals-Centric Approach

Fig. 7.1 Towards a new DNA based

innovative business models that offer superior products and services, ultimately contributing to the betterment of society.

Thus, to conclude, by embedding these principles into their core, enterprises cultivate a holistic and sustainable approach to technological integration. This not only drives their success but also fosters a positive impact on the communities they serve, reinforcing the interconnectedness of business success and societal wellbeing.

This renewed culture, inspired by a conscious knowledge of the new digital paradigm shift with its emphasis on purpose, innovation, and inclusivity, sets the foundation for a future where technology and human values coexist harmoniously, paving the way for a prosperous and equitable society.

Case Insights Box. Leveraging Digital Innovation for Sustainable Development in Local Territorial Systems—The Case Study of TaWave
TaWave, where the term "TA" refers to the city of Taranto and "WAVE" symbolizes the broader concept of innovation as a force that can either overwhelm those who ignore it or be harnessed by those who can take advantage of it, is an innovative event that has contributed—and continues to contribute—positively to the transformation and revitalization of the Taranto area. This area, already perceived with a stereotypical image of its strategic vocation (Golfetto, 1996), is being redefined by such initiatives. The aim of this initiative is to explore whether digital innovation can serve as a driving force for sustainable development within Local Territorial Systems (LTSs).

LTSs are crucial in analysing societal evolution, as they allow for an integrated approach to measuring the impact of innovation and technology on society from a sustainability perspective. In this context, sustainability is not limited to environmental aspects but also encompasses ethical and social dimensions. By focusing on these areas, the contributions of innovation and technology towards enhancing community well-being can be better understood (Guido & Pino, 2010).

The research findings revealed that the TaWave initiative had a positive and significant impact on the community, as evidenced by the participants' feedback and the professional opportunities that emerged. Digital innovation, therefore, can be considered a powerful driver of transformation, change, and revitalization even in Local Territorial Systems that are traditionally associated with different strategic vocations, such as the Taranto area.

Our results identified four main categories of impact generated by TaWave:

Firstly, as for (1) *Awareness and Visibility*, TaWave captured national attention by promoting an image of the Taranto area's Local Territorial System that is oriented towards digital innovation rather than the steel industry, thereby enhancing the area's attractiveness and competitiveness on a national scale. Secondly, as for (2) *Participation and Involvement*, From its very first edition, TaWave achieved remarkable success, as evident from the participation numbers. This success can be largely attributed to the valuable collaboration and synergy with various stakeholders who served as partners and sponsors.

Since its inception, TaWave has benefitted from the support of leading technical partners, who have significantly contributed to the event's success. Additionally, institutional partners, such as the Municipality of Taranto and the University of Bari Aldo Moro, have supported the event. As a unique opportunity to promote digital transformation in Taranto and Apulia, TaWave aligns perfectly with the development strategies of these entities, helping to improve the city's image and making it more attractive to various stakeholders and citizens (Sestino & Guido, 2021).

Subsequently, the Apulia Region, the Ionian Department in Legal and Economic Systems of the Mediterranean Society—Environment—Culture, the Taranto Chamber of Commerce, Confindustria Taranto, and Confcommercio Taranto also joined the initiative. The support from these entities has strengthened TaWave's credibility and expanded its reach, encouraging broader audience participation. Finally, (3) *Encouraging Innovation in Businesses*. Indeed, the collaboration with partners facilitated the sharing of ideas and the initiation of new projects aimed at integrating innovative solutions and technologies to address future challenges. Additionally, the cross-pollination of different business cultures fostered creativity, leading to the emergence of innovative ideas.

Given the current socio-economic conditions, there is an urgent need for local policymakers to reflect on their role in the context of digital and sustainable transformation. This requires the development of an effective Local Territorial System and the implementation of actionable guidelines. Future efforts must converge to guide effective and lasting actions that inspire, disseminate, and popularize the key drivers of digitization and digital, sustainable transformation in contemporary society.

The first step in this process involves designing and implementing awareness campaigns to educate citizens on the importance of digital transformation. These campaigns should utilize multiple communication channels, including traditional media (e.g., billboards, TV, and newspapers) and digital tools (e.g., online campaigns). Policymakers can actively contribute to initiatives and events that spread awareness about digital issues, such as delivering keynote speeches, moderating roundtable discussions, attending networking events, and showcasing innovative projects. In the long term, this could involve signing memoranda of understanding, establishing collaboration agreements, and creating permanent thematic working groups. Moreover, policymakers should create and implement training courses focused on developing digital citizenship skills.

In conclusion, policymakers play a crucial role in promoting digital transformation and maximizing its benefits for all. Collaborating with private enterprises, civil society, and academia is essential to creating a sustainable, digital, and prosperous future.

Mariagrazia Efato, *President of Association SurfHers*, Co-founder of TaWave.

Specialists' perspectives. Venture Capital Efforts and Startups Impact in Contributing to Wellbeing

The intersection of venture capital and startups with advanced technologies is proving transformative for societal well-being. The infusion of venture capital into startups catalyses the development and adoption of innovative technologies, significantly enhancing various aspects of daily life and economic efficiency. Technologies such as artificial intelligence (AI), blockchain, biotechnology, clean technology (CleanTech), and Industry 4.0 solutions are at the forefront of this transformation.

Startups play a critical role in technological advancement, often spearheading the development of cutting-edge solutions. Technologies like AI, blockchain, biotechnology, CleanTech, and Industry 4.0 are reshaping numerous industries, from healthcare to manufacturing. The potential of these technologies to improve productivity and efficiency is monumental, with AI alone projected to have a global economic impact of $2.6 to $4.4 trillion annually by 2040. Venture capital is essential in this dynamic, ensuring a steady flow of funds that enables startups to innovate and bring disruptive solutions to market.

A key aspect of fostering innovation is the efficient transfer of technology from research laboratories to the market. Technology transfer bridges the gap between academia and industry, enabling scientific breakthroughs to be developed into viable products and services. This process is crucial for deep-tech startups, which rely on cutting-edge scientific research. Europe, for instance, boasts several top-ranked universities in computer science and engineering, providing a solid foundation for technological innovation.

Technological advancements have a profound impact on societal well-being. In healthcare, AI and biotechnology are revolutionizing diagnostics, personalized medicine, and treatment development. AI facilitates the analysis of vast datasets, improving the accuracy and speed of medical diagnoses and treatments. Biotechnological innovations, such as gene therapy and regenerative medicine, offer new hope for treating previously incurable diseases.

Investments in AI-driven HealthTech and Life Sciences have surged, focusing on personalized medicine, predictive analytics, and advanced diagnostics. For example, AI can predict epidemic outbreaks and personalize patient care based on genetic data, significantly improving healthcare outcomes.

In Italy, a strategic focus on AI and HealthTech has led to the development of innovative startups such as Sibylla, which uses AI to discover treatments for oncological diseases, and MedLea, which has created a digital twin for pulmonary health. These advancements highlight the symbiotic relationship between venture capital, AI, and enhanced societal well-being.

CleanTech is another critical area where technology positively impacts society. Clean technologies aim to reduce environmental impact through sustainable practices and renewable energy solutions. These advancements contribute to combating climate change and promoting environmental sustainability, ultimately leading to healthier living conditions.

Industry 4.0 technologies, including the Internet of Things (IoT), robotics, and advanced manufacturing, enhance industrial productivity and efficiency. These innovations lead to increased economic output and job creation, thereby improving the overall quality of life. Startups and the venture capital backing them play a major role in economic growth and job creation. Startups are responsible for approximately 20% of employment across OECD countries and create nearly 50% of new jobs annually. This not only stimulates economic activity but also ensures that talent is retained within the region, fostering a robust industrial ecosystem. The combined enterprise value of European startups and unicorns reached €2.5 trillion in 2023, underscoring their economic significance.

Venture capital investments are crucial in maintaining and enhancing industrial competitiveness. Startups often develop technologies that can be integrated into industrial processes, increasing efficiency and productivity. For example, the adoption of Industry 4.0 technologies has led to a 7% increase in labor productivity among firms. This integration of advanced technologies into traditional industries ensures long-term sustainability and economic resilience.

In conclusion, the strategic investment of venture capital into startups focused on a broad range of advanced technologies is significantly impacting societal well-being by driving technological innovation and economic growth. These technologies not only enhance the quality of life through improved healthcare, environmental sustainability, and industrial efficiency but also contribute to economic stability and job creation. As venture capital continues to support the growth and development of startups, the positive feedback loop between technological innovation and societal well-being is expected to strengthen, leading to a more prosperous and technologically advanced society.

Cristina Dachille, *Strategy & Sustainability Manager*, CDP Venture Capital SGR, Rome, Italy.

7.2   Overall Theoretical Implications

This book underscores the profound, multifaceted benefits of digital technologies, highlighting how integrating emotional engagement, ethical frameworks, and sustainable practices into digital innovations can significantly enhance both individual and societal wellbeing.

From a theoretical perspective, the expanded TAM, as proposed in Chapter 3, now incorporates perceived wellbeing, demonstrating that technological adoption is influenced not only by perceived usefulness and ease of use but also by the emotional and psychological benefits users derive from these technologies (Venkatesh & Davis, 2000). This broader perspective enables an understanding of the multifaceted impact of technology on users, particularly in the realm of healthcare.

As observed within mHealth and DTx technologies, the setting of the empirical study in Chapter 3, individuals who experience improvements in their overall quality of life and health through these technological interventions develop a positive attitude towards these tools, increasing their willingness to use them consistently (Hong et al., 2021; Nwosu et al., 2022; Sestino & D'Angelo, 2024). This positive attitude is crucial for the long-term success and sustainability of health technologies. When users perceive that a technology positively impacts their wellbeing, they are more likely to integrate it into their daily routines and adhere to prescribed therapeutic protocols.

The sense of satisfaction and loyalty derived from these healthcare technologies encourages users to engage with them for longer periods and share their positive experiences, which in turn promotes favourable word-of-mouth. This is particularly important in the healthcare sector, where personal recommendations and shared experiences can significantly influence others' willingness to adopt new technologies. Positive word-of-mouth can accelerate the diffusion of these technologies, making them more widely accepted and utilized.

This dynamic suggests that perceived wellbeing acts as an essential mediator in how technology use in therapeutic settings influences subsequent behaviours and communication patterns. When users feel that their wellbeing is enhanced by technology, they are not only more likely to continue using it but also to communicate its benefits to others, thereby creating a positive feedback loop that can drive broader adoption.

The enhanced patient outcomes and engagement observed with mHealth and DTx technologies highlight the pivotal role of these digital health interventions in improving overall healthcare experiences. These technologies offer more than just functional benefits; they contribute to a holistic sense of wellbeing that encompasses physical, emotional, and psychological health. By addressing these diverse aspects of wellbeing, mHealth and DTx technologies can foster deeper user satisfaction and stronger long-term adherence to therapeutic protocols.

Another important theoretical contribution is to the PERMA model. In the context of the PERMA model (Seligman, 2011; 2018), which emphasizes the enhancement of wellbeing through positive emotions, engagement, relationships, meaning, and accomplishment, the deployment of AR in cultural heritage sites, as presented in Chapter 5, serves as a prime example of technology's role in enriching user experiences. This approach is well illustrated by the integration of AR to facilitate immersive educational experiences that are not only informative but also highly engaging. The utilization of AR and VR in these settings, as explored in studies by Huang and Soman (2013) and Ibáñez et colleagues (2020), has been shown to significantly increase visitor satisfaction by making learning more interactive and enjoyable.

Adding to this, the gamification of such experiences (Koivisto & Hamari, 2019; Sailer et al., 2017) further amplifies enjoyment and engagement, thereby enhancing life satisfaction. Gamification transforms traditional visits into dynamic, interactive encounters, making AR interfaces more intuitive and beneficial, thus increasing the perceived ease of use and usefulness of the technology. Visitors find these interfaces engaging and enjoyable, encouraging repeat visits and promoting the educational potential of AR.

This positive perception is crucial in fostering a sense of accomplishment and meaning, aligning with the core principles of the PERMA model. By integrating AR and VR into cultural heritage sites, visitors can form deeper connections with the content, enhancing their relationships with the subject matter and with other visitors. These technologies create a shared experience that fosters community and collective learning, contributing to the overall wellbeing of visitors.

Ultimately, AR and VR technologies contribute to a richer, more satisfying visitor experience that aligns with the PERMA model's core principles. They offer an innovative way to engage visitors, making learning more enjoyable and impactful, thus promoting a positive and fulfilling experience that enhances both individual and collective wellbeing. This alignment with the PERMA model underscores the importance of considering emotional and psychological benefits in the adoption and sustained use of educational technologies, leading to more effective and user-centred interventions in cultural heritage settings.

In the realm of digital entertainment, the concept of affective computing (Picard, 2000), where AI systems are designed to recognize, interpret, and simulate human emotions, underscores the importance of emotional engagement (Juslin & Västfjäll, 2008; De Witte et al., 2022). As exhibited in Chapter 4, AI-driven recommendation systems in music streaming services exemplify how emotional connectivity can foster deeper user trust and sustained engagement. This illustrates how technological interfaces shape user perceptions and emotional responses.

AI systems in music streaming services leverage user data to create personalized recommendations that resonate with individual emotional states and preferences. By curating playlists that align with users' moods, these systems enhance the overall listening experience, making it more enjoyable and relevant. This personalization not only meets practical needs by offering convenient and efficient access to preferred content but also addresses psychological needs by providing an emotionally gratifying experience.

Moreover, the ability of AI to adapt and evolve based on user feedback further strengthens this emotional bond. As users interact with these systems, they perceive an increased level of attentiveness and responsiveness, which enhances their trust and satisfaction. When users feel understood and valued, they are more likely to develop a positive attitude towards the technology, leading to higher levels of sustained engagement and loyalty.

The impact of affective computing extends beyond individual user experiences to influence broader user behaviour patterns. By fostering a sense of emotional connection, AI systems encourage users to spend more time on the platform, explore new content, and share their experiences with others. This creates a positive feedback loop where increased engagement leads to more data, which in turn allows for even more accurate and emotionally attuned recommendations.

Additionally, the integration of affective computing in digital entertainment can also enhance social connections among users. Features such as shared playlists and collaborative filtering enable users to connect with others who have similar tastes and emotional responses to music. This fosters a sense of community and shared emotional experiences, further enriching the user experience.

By addressing both practical and psychological needs, AI systems not only improve user satisfaction but also contribute to a more profound and lasting relationship between users and the technology. When users perceive that an AI system understands and responds to their emotional states, their trust in the system increases. This heightened trust leads to higher levels of sustained engagement and loyalty, as users become more invested in a technology that consistently meets their emotional and practical needs.

However, alongside the benefits of personalized and digital user experiences, privacy, security, and ethical considerations remain critical themes across all domains. Ensuring the positive adoption and sustainable integration of digital technologies necessitates effectively managing these concerns to mitigate user apprehensions and foster trust (Wang et al., 2018).

The integration of ethical considerations, particularly in healthcare and AI applications, is crucial for maintaining user trust and promoting the sustainable adoption of digital technologies. The protection of personal data and ethical use of technology, as highlighted by Lee and Kim (2018) and Park and Lee (2020), directly influence user acceptance and overall wellbeing. Managing privacy and security concerns effectively is essential to foster a trusted environment where users feel safe and valued.

This balance is also reflected in the broader societal impact of SDBMs within the healthcare sector. As offered in Chapter 6, Platforms like Pyllola integrate environmental, social, and economic sustainability into their operations, illustrating how digital tools can transcend traditional barriers to healthcare access and promote resource efficiency (Bocken et al., 2014; Schaltegger & Burritt, 2018). Theories from sustainability and business model innovation highlight the dual benefits of these digital platforms: addressing immediate healthcare needs while also achieving long-term sustainability goals (Oderanti et al., 2021; Sestino et al., 2024). By embedding sustainability into their core operations, these platforms demonstrate how digital innovations can support not only individual well-being but also broader societal and environmental objectives. This holistic approach ensures that the benefits of digital health technologies extend beyond individual users to positively impact the community and the environment, reinforcing the importance of integrating ethical considerations and sustainable practices in the development and deployment of digital technologies.

7.3   STRATEGIC AND MANAGERIAL IMPLICATIONS

The empirical studies presented in this book offer substantial insights into the strategic implementation of advanced technologies, highlighting their potential to create differentiation, achieve competitive advantage, and explore new markets through innovative approaches.

In the healthcare sector, the adoption of mobile health technologies that enhance perceived wellbeing offers a powerful differentiation strategy. As shown in Chapter 3, healthcare providers that implement user-friendly, beneficial digital tools can significantly improve patient quality of life by making technologies intuitive and easily accessible, ensuring that patients of all ages and technological proficiency can use them effectively. This ease of use is critical for consistent engagement and adherence to treatment plans. Furthermore, these advanced digital tools can lead to significant reductions in healthcare costs. By improving patient adherence to treatment plans and enabling early detection of potential health issues, these technologies help prevent complications and reduce the need for more intensive and expensive interventions. This proactive approach to healthcare management is both cost-effective and beneficial for patient outcomes.

Similarly, in the realm of music services, AI-driven recommendation systems utilize emotional intelligence to create a unique competitive edge. As presented in Chapter 4, these systems personalize music to resonate with users' current emotional states, thereby fostering deeper emotional connections and enhancing user satisfaction and trust. By analysing data points such as listening history, time of day, and even biometric data, these platforms tailor music recommendations that align with the user's immediate mood and preferences. This mirrors the healthcare sector's use of technologies to improve patient engagement and outcomes through personalized interventions.

Moreover, just as mobile health technologies continuously adapt to healthcare trends and patient needs, AI-driven music services extend their personalization capabilities beyond mere suggestions. By integrating advanced machine learning techniques, these platforms can predict and adapt to subtle changes in a user's preferences and emotional state over time, much like healthcare systems adapt to patient feedback and evolving medical standards. For instance, if a user typically listens to upbeat music during workouts and calming music in the evenings, the system can dynamically adjust to these patterns and provide the most appropriate music at the right moments.

The emotional resonance achieved through these personalized recommendations plays a crucial role in both sectors. In healthcare, engaging technologies ensure better patient outcomes and satisfaction; in music streaming, they enhance user retention and loyalty by meeting emotional and musical needs in real-time. This capability to cater to emotional states can be a significant competitive advantage, distinguishing music services in a crowded market where many platforms offer similar libraries but lack emotionally intelligent interactions. Developers and managers in both industries should therefore prioritize emotional aspects in their technological solutions to enhance user experiences and maintain a competitive edge.

The innovative use of digital technologies is not limited to healthcare and music but extends into the cultural heritage sector. As shown in Chapter 5, the use of AR and gamification in cultural heritage exemplifies a blue ocean strategy, where innovative technologies create new market spaces by making the competition irrelevant. The application of the four actions framework (eliminate, reduce, increase, and create) helps cultural heritage managers design AR applications that are both user-friendly and engaging, attracting tech-savvy younger audiences and transforming passive visits into active, immersive experiences.

First, by applying the *eliminate* action, cultural heritage sites can remove elements that are less appealing to visitors. For instance, eliminating traditional static displays in favour of dynamic AR experiences can capture the interest of a modern audience that seeks interactive and engaging content.

Second, the *reduce* action can be applied by minimizing the barriers to visitor engagement. This might include simplifying the user interface of AR applications to ensure they are intuitive and easy to use for all age groups, thereby reducing the learning curve and increasing immediate engagement.

Third, the *increase* action involves enhancing aspects of the visitor experience that provide greater value. By incorporating gamification elements such as rewards, challenges, and interactive storytelling, cultural heritage sites can significantly raise the level of visitor satisfaction. For example, visitors might use AR apps to embark on treasure hunts, solving puzzles, and discovering hidden facts about exhibits as they progress. This interactive approach makes learning about history more engaging and memorable, catering to the expectations of modern audiences.

Finally, the *create* action focuses on introducing new features that were previously unavailable. AR can be used to recreate historical scenes, allowing visitors to witness historical events as if they were there. This immersive experience provides a more vivid and memorable understanding of history compared to traditional exhibits. Additionally, AR applications can offer multi-language support, making the site more accessible to international visitors and enhancing their overall experience.

By implementing these four actions, cultural heritage sites can differentiate themselves and open new avenues for visitor interaction and education. Gamified experiences often encourage social interactions, as visitors can compete with friends or share their achievements on social media, further promoting the site. This strategy not only makes the cultural heritage sites more attractive but also ensures repeat visits and long-term engagement.

Returning to the health sector, the study on sustainable digital business models underscores the substantial innovation advantages that digital platforms provide. As highlighted in Chapter 6, platforms like Pyllola exemplify how digital means can expand service reach and improve patient care. These platforms leverage technology to make healthcare services more accessible, especially in underserved or remote areas, thus bridging gaps in healthcare delivery and ensuring that a larger population can benefit from essential medical services.

Moreover, the innovation advantage provided by digital platforms addresses immediate healthcare needs efficiently. During crises, such as the COVID-19 pandemic, digital health solutions have proven invaluable. They enabled continued access to healthcare while minimizing the risk of infection through remote consultations and monitoring.

In addition to immediate benefits, digital platforms also position healthcare providers to better handle future crises. By establishing robust digital infrastructures, providers can ensure continuity of care even when traditional healthcare delivery methods are disrupted. This proactive approach not only prepares the healthcare system for emergencies but also enhances overall resilience and capacity to deal with unexpected challenges.

Furthermore, digital platforms contribute to cost efficiencies in healthcare delivery. They can reduce operational costs by streamlining administrative processes, decreasing the need for physical infrastructure, and optimizing resource allocation. These savings can be redirected towards improving patient care and investing in further technological advancements, creating a cycle of continuous improvement and innovation.

Supportive regulatory frameworks play an undeniably crucial role in this scenario. Indeed, regulatory support can streamline the approval process for new technologies, ensure data privacy and security, and provide guidelines that help maintain the quality and reliability of digital health services. This supportive environment is crucial for fostering innovation and allowing digital platforms to thrive.

In conclusion, this book offers numerous insights at the strategic and management levels. The integration of advanced technologies into strategic planning is essential for achieving differentiation and gaining a competitive advantage. By emphasizing innovation, user-centric design, and sustainable practices, managers can significantly enhance service delivery and secure long-term strategic benefits. This comprehensive approach ensures that organizations not only meet the evolving needs of their stakeholders but also achieve sustained success and leadership in their respective industries.

7.4   Marketing
and Consumers-Related Implications

Based on the studies conducted in the previous chapter, our book may offer significant for both marketers and policymakers.

By focusing on individuals' reactions, our insights may provide a roadmap for companies seeking to align their marketing strategies with evolving consumers' expectations, leveraging digital technologies not just for innovation, but also for improving their wellbeing and, indirectly, the overall societal value.

Based on the findings and discussions presented across the chapters collectively, a transformative approach to marketing and consumer behaviour strategies clearly emerges, and specifically focused on the integration of digital technologies and a renewed focus on consumer wellbeing. As this book states in the introductory chapter, a shift in digital-related strategies is compulsory to better satisfy consumers' needs, coherently with the original firms' purposes. In such a context, emphasizing the need for companies to reconnect with their fundamental purpose is not merely profit generation but—as anticipated—to fulfil consumer needs in a coherent and sustainable manner.

This realignment necessitates that marketing strategies prioritize consumers' satisfaction and value creation over sheer sales volumes. Indeed, in the current society, ethical and moral standards are ever-growing asked by individuals and societies. Thus, marketers should clearly understand the norms and values expected of them and act in a positive, ethical manner. By leveraging new digital technologies, companies may enhance individual and societal wellbeing, thus fostering a sustainable business orientation that is increasingly crucial in today's evolving markets, characterized by—likewise—evolving consumers. Indeed, based on the literature review conducted in Chapter 2, shedding light on the relationship between individual wellbeing and digital technologies, we elucidate how emerging technological trends (e.g., as for IoT, Big Data, VR, AR, and AI), may impact consumer behaviour, particularly in sectors like healthcare, tourism, music, and cultural heritage. The insights drawn from this qualitative study resulting as a review, not only drove the authors in designing the studies presented in the subsequent chapters, but immediately also suggested that marketing strategies, today, must incorporate these technologies to design experiences, not only mainly directed to satisfy consumers' needs but also positively influence their positive emotional and psychological effects, as a fundamentals part of the omni-comprehensive "wellbeing" concept.

When focusing on the study related to mobile health technologies (Chapter 3), these insights are evident. In that study, we did not focus on the final outcomes of the treatment, but we focused on patients-as-consumers' individual differences to sage how this individual characteristic may shape their further behaviour. Indeed, we demonstrate that the integration of digital tools significantly enhances patients' engagement and positive word-of-mouth, mediated by perceived wellbeing. Thus, marketers in the healthcare sector should focus on promoting the benefits of these technologies, emphasizing their role in improving health outcomes and enhancing patients' satisfaction. For instance, marketing and communication campaigns should be also directed to emphasize the experientable wellbeing deriving from the use of DTx and mobile health, to incentivize such technologies' adoption. For instance, because of such results, marketing campaign (and policy campaign, by considering the nature of the research setting) designed for mobile health as digital therapeutics could focus on how these tools empower users to actively manage their wellbeing. Such campaigns may also highlight the ease of access to personalized health plans, tracking progress, and receiving real-time feedback via mobile apps. Importantly, communication strategies could also emphasize the convenience of integrating these digital solutions into daily routines, enhancing overall perceivable wellbeing.

When considering another important setting, that is the music industry, Chapter 4 interestingly shed light on the crucial role of Artificial Intelligence technologies, and the crucial role of individuals' positive emotions (as a subdimension of the construct of individuals' wellbeing, based on the PERMA scale; Seligman, 2018). The AI-based music recommendation systems reinforce the importance of perceived ease of use and perceived usefulness in fostering positive emotional responses and trust in AI tools. Indeed, both perceived ease of use and usefulness positively affect individuals' positive emotions, and in turn, their positive behaviour. This result is crucial for marketers, since future marketing strategies should therefore highlight these aspects, showcasing how AI enhances the consumers' experience, particularly in emotionally driven industries (like the music one). Indeed, marketing literature (Bagozzi et al., 1999; Davis, 1989), has seminally and long demonstrated how positive emotions act as antecedents of positive behaviours, e.g., as for purchase intention or, as in the analysed cases, intention to use new technological (or new technology-based tools).

Similar results are observed in leisure-related domains. For instance, recent studies (Amatulli et al., 2021) have demonstrated that certain types of tourism activities can positively influence life satisfaction and individual wellbeing, even in contexts enriched by new technologies that support such experiences (e.g., as in Eryılmaz et al., 2021). This positive impact is also attributed to the activation of emotional factors. Coherently, Chapter 5, by focusing on the exploration of AR and gamification tools, in cultural heritage experiences further supports the reasoning about the positive exploitation of new technologies to boost both individuals' experiences, and elements "composing" their perceivable wellbeing, finally suggesting findings for immersive and engaging marketing strategies.

Importantly, Chapter 5 focuses on the crucial role of individuals' enjoyment (part of the wellbeing subdimension as well; Seligman, 2011; 2018). Based on our findings, integrating gamification elements could significantly increase consumers' engagement and the perceived educational value of products or services, ultimately leading to higher life satisfaction, because of the ancient role of their enjoyment. This insight is particularly valuable for industries where education and entertainment overlap, as it suggests that gamified experiences can enhance consumer involvement and satisfaction. Thus, in designing such experiences marketers should empathize the experientable enjoyment. For instance, marketing campaign may emphasize the thrill of exploring heritage sites through AR, unlocking stories and artifacts via gamified challenges. Moreover, such campaigns could also showcase the blend of education and entertainment, making history "engaging" and accessible. Furthermore, marketers may also act in improving the personalized journey that each visitor could experience, deepening their connection to the cultural narrative, making it more enjoyable.

Finally, the reasoning about the crucial role of sustainable digital business models presented in Chapter 6, suggests how digital ecosystem should be built by leveraging new platform in order to offer new kinds of services to the final consumers, indirectly impacting on their need for satisfaction and wellbeing. The digital platform like the one analysed in Chapter 6, not only may serve a specific "native" market segment (e.g., Italian patients seeking telemedicine), but could also expand into the market segment of tourists in Italy or those who cannot physically access healthcare services (e.g., by going in closer hospitals, clinics, and so on). On one hand, the company taps into new market segments by breaking down geographical barriers, and on the other, there are multiple benefits for the end users. For example, the case study highlights how foreign patients can conveniently access prescription services and tele-consultations within Italy through the platform, rather than having to visit the nearest hospital in person. In this sense, marketing communications should thus emphasize the firms' commitment to sustainability and its positive social impact, resonating with the growing consumer demand for ethical business practices. Furthermore, marketing and advertising campaigns could also underline the convenience of accessing quality care remotely, leveraging digital technology (i.e., the employed digital platform), and user-friendly interfaces.

Thus, in conclusion, from a marketing perspective, the book provides multiple insights for marketing and communication campaigns, as it acknowledges the crucial role of the features of new technologies and balances with individuals (such as general consumers, patients, tourists, and so on), importantly considering the various components that can lead to an increased perception of wellbeing (e.g., emotional, psychological, social, and affective aspects) as well.

7.5   Conclusions and Final Remarks

7.5.1   *Conclusion*

In the contemporary era, new technologies hold a crucial role.

The various generational cohorts that populate the world, regardless of their individual objectives, cannot help but embrace digital technologies as an integral part of their daily lives. In this pervasive context, characterized more than ever by the rapid evolution of artificial intelligence, the positive effort of enterprises should be directed towards integrating these technologies.

This integration is not only to enhance the decision-making process by making it more accurate and informed, but also to restructure their value propositions to end consumers, thereby indirectly benefiting society as a whole. In doing so, the guiding principle should not be solely the pursuit of profit, but rather a commitment to contributing positively to the wellbeing of individuals and society. This entails an improvement in living conditions, a goal that aligns with the current *Sustainable Development Goals* (SDGs), making it even more relevant and necessary.

Throughout this book, we have proposed a new perspective on the "Digital Paradigm Shift", emphasizing the importance of businesses focusing not only on meeting consumer needs, a foundational reason for the existence of enterprises, but more importantly, on pursuing an additional "surplus" value, a sort of "improved" created value.

This "improved" value derives from a new orientation of firms a new DNA and a new vision that is intrinsically linked to perceived wellbeing. We advocate that today's business efforts should be consciously directed towards leveraging new technologies to enhance the quality of life for individuals and society, while also contributing, in some cases, to sustainable development from economic, environmental, ethical, and social perspectives.

Through four exploratory studies, we have shed light on how new technologies can permeate various significant industries and how the perceived wellbeing of the ultimate beneficiaries of business efforts— the consumers, but more broadly, all individuals who "consume" what they require (e.g., goods, services, experiences, and so on)—has a crucial impact on the intention to adopt new technologies. This wellbeing encompasses emotional, psychological, and social benefits, which are essential components of a modern, highly digitalized era characterized by the hyper-personalization of offerings.

The evidence presented in these studies underscores that the adoption of new technologies is not merely a matter of functionality or convenience but is deeply intertwined with the wellbeing of individuals. This realization calls for a shift in the way businesses approach technology integration. Enterprises should view technological advancements as tools to foster greater emotional and psychological satisfaction, thereby aligning their objectives with broader societal goals.

As we conclude this journey through the digital transformation landscape, it becomes evident that the role of technology extends far beyond operational efficiency or competitive advantage. It is a pivotal factor in shaping the future of human experiences and societal progress. By adopting a holistic approach that prioritizes wellbeing and sustainable development, businesses can not only thrive in the digital age but also contribute meaningfully to the betterment of society. This is the essence of the "Digital Paradigm Shift" we envision, a future where technology serves humanity, enhancing lives and fostering a sustainable world for generations to come.

7.5.2 Final Remarks and Proposal for Future Research

To conclude, as we deeply underlined in this book, by considering the current area marked by continuous technological advancement, it is imperative that the adoption and implementation of new technologies are not solely directed towards meeting immediate needs but are also geared towards enhancing the overall wellbeing of individuals and society.

Such a "broad" concept of wellbeing should be conceptualized "holistically", and thus by encompassing not only material and monetary aspects but also psychological and social dimensions.

Indeed, the variety and the potentialities of the new emerging technologies present unprecedented opportunities to elevate the quality of life by fostering community cohesion, mental health, and social inclusion. Therefore, it is desirable for there to be a collective commitment to utilizing technologies in a manner guided by ethical principles and a long-term vision, wherein technological progress is harmonized with human and social advancement.

Based on the results of this book, and by considering the current scenario, future research should explore several critical areas to better understand and maximize the positive impacts of technology on wellbeing.

From a managerial perspective, for instance, it is essential to investigate how organizations could integrate technological governance practices that not only maximize profit, but also promote social wellbeing, aligning with social, environmental, and ethical goals. For instance, future research could focus on how organizations could develop internal policies that encourage the adoption of technologies fostering inclusion, diversity, and employee wellbeing, and evaluate the long-term impact of such policies on organizational performance, and—indirectly—on individuals and societies.

Another plea, related to another relevant area of study could be the role of ethical leadership in steering technological innovation. Indeed "good" firms, organizations, and so on, "derive" from good managers and leaders. Thus, by examining how leaders may influence organizational culture to support the adoption of technologies that are not only efficient but also socially responsible may provide insights into how such approaches affect corporate reputation and stakeholder trust.

From a marketing and consumer perspective, future research could explore how social and ethical marketing (intended as managerial efforts oriented to the market), may be enhanced by digital technologies to promote behaviours that improve psychological and social wellbeing and lifestyle. For instance, investigating the use of current "trend" technologies like Artificial Intelligence, to disseminate awareness campaigns on topics such as mental health, sustainability, and inclusion could vintage valuable insights into effectiveness and long-term impact. Additionally, further exploration should be directed at investigating how newer consumer experience may be designed when mediated by the pervasive integration of digital technologies, and how such experiences can be optimized to provide not only functional value but also psychological and social value, contributing to a positive wellbeing state. Moreover, research could also explore the concept of emotional value generated through technological interactions and its impact on consumers' loyalty and overall wellbeing.

Our "hope", at the end of this book is that managers, marketers, and firms understand the relevance of promoting and boosting individuals' wellbeing to positively contribute and positively shape a better future for the society as a whole, and that future research efforts will focus in understanding how technologies may be harnessed as a vehicle for advancing wellbeing, as a concept that extends beyond material dimensions, embracing an integrated vision of human and social progress.

Declaration of Interest   The authors declare no competing interests.

Declaration of Generative AI and AI-Assisted Technologies in the Writing Process   During the preparation of this book, the authors used AI tools (i.e., Chat GPT) and Grammarly only for proof reading purposes, and thus only to check grammar, in order to improve language and readability. After using these tools, the authors reviewed and edited the content as needed and take full responsibility for the content of the publication.

REFERENCES

Abuhassna, H., Al-Rahmi, W. M., Yahya, N., Zakaria, M. A. Z. M., Kosnin, A. B. M., & Darwish, M. (2020). Development of a new model on utilizing online learning platforms to improve students' academic achievements and satisfaction. *International Journal of Educational Technology in Higher Education, 17*, 1–23.

Acciarini, C., Boccardelli, P., & Brunetta, F. (2024). *Leadership and Transformation*. In Leadership and Strategic Management (pp. 43–56). Routledge.

Afchar, D., Melchiorre, A., Schedl, M., Hennequin, R., Epure, E., & Moussallam, M. (2022). Explainability in music recommender systems. *AI Magazine, 43*(2), 190–208.

Afsar, M. M., Crump, T., & Far, B. (2022). Reinforcement learning based recommender systems: A survey. *ACM Computing Surveys, 55*(7), 1–38.

Agatz, N., Erera, A., Savelsbergh, M., & Wang, X. (2012). Optimization for dynamic ride-sharing: A review. *European Journal of Operational Research, 223*(2), 295–303.

Ajzen, I., & Fishbein, M. (1975). A Bayesian analysis of attribution processes. *Psychological Bulletin, 82*(2), 261.

Ajzen, I., & Fishbein, M. (2000). Attitudes and the attitude-behavior relation: Reasoned and automatic processes. *European Review of Social Psychology, 11*(1), 1–33.

Akçayır, M., & Akçayır, G. (2017). Advantages and challenges associated with augmented reality for education: A systematic review of the literature. *Educational Research Review, 20*, 1–11.

© The Editor(s) (if applicable) and The Author(s), under exclusive license to Springer Nature Switzerland AG 2025
A. Sestino and L. Nasta, *The Digital Paradigm Shift for a New Business DNA*, https://doi.org/10.1007/978-3-031-76238-3

Akhgar, B., Saathoff, G. B., Arabnia, H. R., Hill, R., Staniforth, A., & Bayerl, P. S. (2015). *Application of big data for national security: A practitioner's guide to emerging technologies.* Butterworth-Heinemann.

Alam, M. Z., Alam, M. M. D., Uddin, M. A., & Mohd Noor, N. A. (2022). Do mobile health (mHealth) services ensure the quality of health life? An integrated approach from a developing country context. *Journal of Marketing Communications, 28*(2), 152–182.

Alqahtani, A. (2015). Towards a framework for the potential cyber-terrorist threat to critical national infrastructure: A quantitative study. *Information & Computer Security, 23*(5), 532–569.

Alsawaier, R. S. (2018). The effect of gamification on motivation and engagement. *The International Journal of Information and Learning Technology, 35*(1), 56–79.

Amatulli, C., Peluso, A. M., Sestino, A., Petruzzellis, L., & Guido, G. (2021). The role of psychological flow in adventure tourism: Sociodemographic antecedents and consequences on word-of-mouth and life satisfaction. *Journal of Sport & Tourism, 25*(4), 353–369.

Amit, R., & Zott, C. (2015). Crafting business architecture: The antecedents of business model design. *Strategic Entrepreneurship Journal, 9*(4), 331–350.

Anderson, A., Maystre, L., Anderson, I., Mehrotra, R., & Lalmas, M. (2020, April). Algorithmic effects on the diversity of consumption on spotify. In *Proceedings of the web conference 2020* (pp. 2155–2165).

Antunes, E., Alcaire, R., & Amaral, I. (2022). Wellbeing and (mental) health: A quantitative exploration of Portuguese young adults' uses of M-Apps from a gender perspective. *Social Sciences, 12*(1), 3.

Assuncao, W. G., Piccolo, L. S., & Zaina, L. A. (2022). Considering emotions and contextual factors in music recommendation: A systematic literature review. *Multimedia Tools and Applications, 81*(6), 8367–8407.

Bacca Acosta, J. L., Baldiris Navarro, S. M., Fabregat Gesa, R., & Graf, S. (2014). Augmented reality trends in education: a systematic review of research and applications. *Journal of Educational Technology and Society, 2014, vol. 17, núm. 4, p. 133–149.*

Baer, M., & Frese, M. (2003). Innovation is not enough: Climates for initiative and psychological safety, process innovations, and firm performance. *Journal of Organizational Behavior: The International Journal of Industrial, Occupational and Organizational Psychology and Behavior, 24*(1), 45–68.

Bagozzi, R. P., Gopinath, M., & Nyer, P. U. (1999). The role of emotions in marketing. *Journal of the Academy of Marketing Science, 27*(2), 184–206.

Balta, M., Valsecchi, R., Papadopoulos, T., & Bourne, D. J. (2021). Digitalization and co-creation of healthcare value: A case study in Occupational Health. *Technological Forecasting and Social Change, 168,* 120785.

Bandura, A. (2006). Guide for constructing self-efficacy scales. *Self-Efficacy Beliefs of Adolescents, 5*(1), 307–337.

Barbosa, W., Zhou, K., Waddell, E., Myers, T., & Dorsey, E. R. (2021). Improving access to care: Telemedicine across medical domains. *Annual Review of Public Health, 42*, 463–481.

Barney, J. (1991). Special theory forum the resource-based model of the firm: Origins, implications, and prospects. *Journal of Management, 17*(1), 97–98.

Barney, J. B., Ketchen, D. J., Jr., & Wright, M. (2021). Bold voices and new opportunities: An expanded research agenda for the resource-based view. *Journal of Management, 47*(7), 1677–1683.

Barth, H., Ulvenblad, P., Ulvenblad, P. O., & Hoveskog, M. (2021). Unpacking sustainable business models in the Swedish agricultural sector–the challenges of technological, social and organisational innovation. *Journal of Cleaner Production, 304*, 127004.

Barton, A. J. (2012). The regulation of mobile health applications. *BMC Medicine, 10*, 1–4.

Baudier, P., Kondrateva, G., Ammi, C., Chang, V., & Schiavone, F. (2021). Patients' perceptions of teleconsultation during COVID-19: A cross-national study. *Technological Forecasting and Social Change, 163*, 120510.

Baydas, O., & Cicek, M. (2019). The examination of the gamification process in undergraduate education: A scale development study. *Technology, Pedagogy and Education, 28*(3), 269–285.

Belk, R. W. (2017). Qualitative research in advertising. *Journal of Advertising, 46*(1), 36–47.

Bell, R. G., & Russell, C. (2002). Environmental policy for developing countries. *Issues in Science and Technology, 18*(3), 63–70.

Ben Sassi, I., & Ben Yahia, S. (2021). How does context influence music preferences: A user-based study of the effects of contextual information on users' preferred music. *Multimedia Systems, 27*(2), 143–160.

Bennett, J., & Lanning, S. (2007, August). The Netflix prize. In *Proceedings of KDD cup and workshop* (Vol. 2007, p. 35).

Benyam, A. A., Soma, T., & Fraser, E. (2021). Digital agricultural technologies for food loss and waste prevention and reduction: Global trends, adoption opportunities and barriers. *Journal of Cleaner Production, 323*, 129099.

Bhavnani, S. P., Narula, J., & Sengupta, P. P. (2016). Mobile technology and the digitization of healthcare. *European Heart Journal, 37*(18), 1428.

BIS Research. (August 16, 2018). Augmented reality (AR) market size worldwide in 2017, 2018 and 2025 (in billion U.S. dollars) [Graph]. In *Statista*. Retrieved July 10, 2024, from https://www.statista.com/statistics/897587/world-augmented-reality-market-value/

Blayone, T. J., vanOostveen, R., Barber, W., DiGiuseppe, M., & Childs, E. (2017). Democratizing digital learning: Theorizing the fully online learning community model. *International Journal of Educational Technology in Higher Education, 14*, 1–16.

Bobadilla, J., Ortega, F., Hernando, A., & Gutiérrez, A. (2013). Recommender Systems Survey. *Knowledge-Based Systems, 46*, 109–132.

Boccardelli, P. (2018). Leader for a new world. In Il manager del futuro: scenari, strategie e competenze (pp. 9–31). Fondirigenti G. Taliercio.

Boccardelli, P., & Brunetta, F. (2024). *Leadership and Strategic Management: Decision-Making in Times of Change.* Taylor & Francis.

Boccoli, G., Sestino, A., Gastaldi, L., & Corso, M. (2022). The impact of autonomy and temporal flexibility on individuals' psychological wellbeing in remote settings. *Sinergie – Italian Journal of Management, 40*(2), 327–349.

Boccoli, G., Gastaldi, L., & Corso, M. (2023). The evolution of employee engagement: Towards a social and contextual construct for balancing individual performance and wellbeing dynamically. *International Journal of Management Reviews, 25*(1), 75–98.

Bocken, N. M., Short, S. W., Rana, P., & Evans, S. (2014). A literature and practice review to develop sustainable business model archetypes. *Journal of Cleaner Production, 65*, 42–56.

Boeren, E. (2016). *Lifelong learning participation in a changing policy context: An interdisciplinary theory.* Palgrave Macmillan.

Bontridder, N., & Poullet, Y. (2021). The role of artificial intelligence in disinformation. *Data & Policy, 3*, e32.

Boons, F., Montalvo, C., Quist, J., & Wagner, M. (2013). Sustainable innovation, business models and economic performance: An overview. *Journal of Cleaner Production, 45*, 1–8.

Boulard, T., Montero, J. I., Bakker, J. C., & Adams, S. R. (2007, October). Innovative technologies for an efficient use of energy. In International Symposium on High Technology for Greenhouse System Management: Greensys2007 801 (pp. 49–62).

Bounfour, A. (2016). Digital futures, digital transformation. *Progress in IS, 10*, 978–973.

Bozzelli, G., Raia, A., Ricciardi, S., De Nino, M., Barile, N., Perrella, M., & Palombini, A. (2019). An integrated VR/AR framework for user-centric interactive experience of cultural heritage: The ArkaeVision project. *Digital Applications in Archaeology and Cultural Heritage, 15*, e00124.

Braun, V., & Clarke, V. (2006). Using thematic analysis in psychology. *Qualitative Research in Psychology, 3*(2), 77–101.

Bresciani, S., Ferraris, A., Romano, M., & Santoro, G. (2021a). Digital leadership. In *Digital Transformation Management for Agile Organizations: A Compass to Sail the Digital World* (pp. 97–115). Emerald Publishing Limited.

Bresciani, S., Huarng, K. H., Malhotra, A., & Ferraris, A. (2021b). Digital transformation as a springboard for product, process and business model innovation. *Journal of Business Research, 128*, 204–210.

Brezing, C. A., & Brixner, D. I. (2022). The rise of prescription digital therapeutics in behavioral health. *Advances in Therapy, 39*(12), 5301–5306.

Browne, S. H., Peloquin, C., Santillo, F., Haubrich, R., Muttera, L., Moser, K., & Blaschke, T. F. (2018). Digitizing medicines for remote capture of oral medication adherence using co-encapsulation. *Clinical Pharmacology & Therapeutics, 103*(3), 502–510.

Bruinsma, J. (2017). *World agriculture: Towards 2015/2030: An FAO study.* Routledge.

Brusila, J., Cloonan, M., & Ramstedt, K. (2022). Music, digitalization, and democracy. *Popular Music and Society, 45*(1), 1–12.

Bugeja, M., & Grech, E. M. (2020). Using technology and gamification as a means of enhancing users' experience at cultural heritage sites. *Rediscovering Heritage Through Technology: A Collection of Innovative Research Case Studies That Are Reworking The Way We Experience Heritage*, 69–89.

Bulaj, G., Clark, J., Ebrahimi, M., & Bald, E. (2021). From precision metaphar-macology to patient empowerment: Delivery of self-care practices for epilepsy, pain, depression and cancer using digital health technologies. *Frontiers in Pharmacology, 12*, 612602.

Busby, J. W., Cook, K. H., Vizy, E. K., Smith, T. G., & Bekalo, M. (2014). Identifying hot spots of security vulnerability associated with climate change in Africa. *Climatic Change, 124*, 717–731.

Butler, J., & Kern, M. L. (2016). The PERMA-Profiler: A brief multidimensional measure of flourishing. *International Journal of Wellbeing, 6*(3).

Cainelli, G., D'Amato, A., & Mazzanti, M. (2015). Adoption of waste-reducing technology in manufacturing: Regional factors and policy issues. *Resource and Energy Economics, 39*, 53–67.

Capolongo, S., Gola, M., Di Noia, M., Nickolova, M., Nachiero, D., Rebecchi, A., & Buffoli, M. (2016). Social sustainability in healthcare facilities: A rating tool for analysing and improving social aspects in environments of care. *Annali Dell'istituto Superiore di Sanita, 52*(1), 15–23.

Cardinale, B. J., Duffy, J. E., Gonzalez, A., Hooper, D. U., Perrings, C., Venail, P., & Naeem, S. (2012). Biodiversity loss and its impact on humanity. *Nature, 486*(7401), 59–67.

Carl, J. R., Jones, D. J., Lindhiem, O. J., Doss, B. D., Weingardt, K. R., Timmons, A. C., & Comer, J. S. (2022). Regulating digital therapeu-tics for mental health: Opportunities, challenges, and the essential role of psychologists. *British Journal of Clinical Psychology, 61*, 130–135.

Carole, K. S., Armand, T. P. T., & Kim, H. C. (2024, February). Enhanced Experiences: Benefits of AI-Powered Recommendation Systems. In *2024*

26th International Conference on Advanced Communications Technology (ICACT) (pp. 216–220). IEEE.

Carrera, A., Zoccarato, F., Mazzeo, M., Lettieri, E., Toletti, G., Bertoli, S., & Fresa, E. (2023). What drives patients' acceptance of Digital Therapeutics? Establishing a new framework to measure the interplay between rational and institutional factors. *BMC Health Services Research, 23*(1), 145.

Celma, O. (2010). *Music Recommendation and Discovery: The Long Tail, Long Fail, and Long Play in the Digital Music Space.* Springer.

Cesário, V., & Nisi, V. (2023). Lessons Learned on Engaging Teenage Visitors in Museums with Story-Based and Game-Based Strategies. *ACM Journal on Computing and Cultural Heritage, 16*(2), 1–20.

Chatterjee, R., Ray, R., Dash, S. R., & Jena, O. P. (2021). Conceptualizing tomorrow's healthcare through digitization. Computational Intelligence and Healthcare Informatics, 359–376.

Cheng, A., Ma, D., Pan, Y., & Qian, H. (2023). Enhancing museum visiting experience: investigating the relationships between augmented reality quality, immersion, and TAM using PLS-SEM. *International Journal of Human–Computer Interaction,* 1–12.

Cheng, K. H., & Tsai, C. C. (2013). Affordances of augmented reality in science learning: Suggestions for future research. *Journal of Science Education and Technology, 22,* 449–462.

Cillo, V., Petruzzelli, A. M., Ardito, L., & Del Giudice, M. (2019). Understanding sustainable innovation: A systematic literature review. *Corporate Social Responsibility and Environmental Management, 26*(5), 1012–1025.

Clarke, R. A., & Knake, R. (2019). The internet freedom league. *Foreign Affairs, 98*(5), 184–192.

Colin, C., Prince, V., Bensoussan, J. L., & Picot, M. C. (2023). Music therapy for health workers to reduce stress, mental workload and anxiety: A systematic review. *Journal of Public Health, 45*(3), e532–e541.

Dąbrowska, J., Almpanopoulou, A., Brem, A., Chesbrough, H., Cucino, V., Di Minin, A., & Ritala, P. (2022). Digital transformation, for better or worse: A critical multi-level research agenda. *R&D Management, 52*(5), 930–954.

Damala, A., Cubaud, P., Bationo, A., Houlier, P., & Marchal, I. (2008, September). Bridging the gap between the digital and the physical: design and evaluation of a mobile augmented reality guide for the museum visit. In *Proceedings of the 3rd international conference on Digital Interactive Media in Entertainment and Arts* (pp. 120–127).

Dang, A., Arora, D., & Rane, P. (2020). Role of digital therapeutics and the changing future of healthcare. *Journal of Family Medicine and Primary Care, 9*(5), 2207–2213.

Davis, F. D. (1989). Perceived usefulness, perceived ease of use, and user acceptance of information technology. *MIS Quarterly,* 319–340.

Davis, F. D., & Venkatesh, V. (1996). A critical assessment of potential measurement biases in the technology acceptance model: Three experiments. *International Journal of Human-Computer Studies, 45*(1), 19–45.

Davis, S., & Wiedenbeck, S. (2001). The mediating effects of intrinsic motivation, ease of use and usefulness perceptions on performance in first-time and subsequent computer users. *Interacting with Computers, 13*(5), 549–580.

De Korte, E. M., Wiezer, N., Janssen, J. H., Vink, P., & Kraaij, W. (2018). Evaluating an mHealth app for health and well-being at work: Mixed-method qualitative study. *JMIR mHealth and uHealth, 6*(3), e6335.

De Witte, M., Pinho, A. D. S., Stams, G. J., Moonen, X., Bos, A. E., & Van Hooren, S. (2022). Music therapy for stress reduction: A systematic review and meta-analysis. *Health Psychology Review, 16*(1), 134–159.

Del Giudice, M. (2016). Discovering the Internet of Things (IoT) within the business process management: A literature review on technological revitalization. *Business Process Management Journal, 22*(2), 263–270.

Del Giudice, M., Di Vaio, A., Hassan, R., & Palladino, R. (2022). Digitalization and new technologies for sustainable business models at the ship–port interface: A bibliometric analysis. *Maritime Policy & Management, 49*(3), 410–446.

Deldjoo, Y., Schedl, M., & Knees, P. (2024). Content-driven music recommendation: Evolution, state of the art, and challenges. *Computer Science Review, 51*, 100618.-116.

Deldjoo, Y., Schedl, M., Cremonesi, P., & Pasi, G. (2020). Recommender systems leveraging multimedia content. *ACM Computing Surveys (CSUR), 53*(5), 1–38.

Demir, A. O. (2019). Digital skills, organizational behavior and transformation of human resources: a review. *Ecoforum, 8*(1), 0–0.

Deterding, S., Dixon, D., Khaled, R., & Nacke, L. (2011, September). From game design elements to gamefulness: defining" gamification". In *Proceedings of the 15th international academic MindTrek conference: Envisioning future media environments* (pp. 9–15).

Díaz, S., Settele, J., Brondízio, E. S., Ngo, H. T., Agard, J., Arneth, A., & Zayas, C. N. (2019). Pervasive human-driven decline of life on Earth points to the need for transformative change. *Science, 366*(6471), eaax3100.

Dicheva, D., Dichev, C., Agre, G., & Angelova, G. (2015). Gamification in education: A systematic mapping study. *Journal of Educational Technology & Society, 18*(3), 75–88.

Diener, E., Oishi, S., & Tay, L. (2018). Advances in subjective well-being research. *Nature Human Behaviour, 2*(4), 253–260.

Diener, E., Wirtz, D., Tov, W., Kim-Prieto, C., Choi, D. W., Oishi, S., & Biswas-Diener, R. (2010). New well-being measures: Short scales to assess flourishing and positive and negative feelings. *Social Indicators Research, 97*, 143–156.

Dong, X., Chang, Y., Wang, Y., & Yan, J. (2017). Understanding usage of Internet of Things (IOT) systems in China: Cognitive experience and affect experience as moderator. *Information Technology & People, 30*(1), 117–138.

Doyle, J. P., Filo, K., Lock, D., Funk, D. C., & McDonald, H. (2016). Exploring PERMA in spectator sport: Applying positive psychology to examine the individual-level benefits of sport consumption. *Sport Management Review, 19*(5), 506–519.

Duporge, I., Isupova, O., Reece, S., Macdonald, D. W., & Wang, T. (2021). Using very-high-resolution satellite imagery and deep learning to detect and count African elephants in heterogeneous landscapes. *Remote Sensing in Ecology and Conservation, 7*(3), 369–381.

Duthely, L. M., & Sanchez-Covarrubias, A. P. (2020). Digitized HIV/AIDS treatment adherence interventions: A review of recent SMS/texting mobile health applications and implications for theory and practice. *Frontiers in Communication, 5*, 530164.

Economou, M., & Tost, L. P. (2011). Evaluating the use of virtual reality and multimedia applications for presenting the past. In *Handbook of research on technologies and cultural heritage: Applications and environments* (pp. 223–239). IGI Global.

Eisenberger, R., Huntington, R., Hutchison, S., & Sowa, D. (1986). Perceived organizational support. *Journal of Applied Psychology, 71*(3), 500.

Eisenstadt, M., Liverpool, S., Infanti, E., Ciuvat, R. M., & Carlsson, C. (2021). Mobile apps that promote emotion regulation, positive mental health, and well-being in the general population: Systematic review and meta-analysis. *JMIR Mental Health, 8*(11), e31170.

Ekeland, A. G., Bowes, A., & Flottorp, S. (2010). Effectiveness of telemedicine: A systematic review of reviews. *International Journal of Medical Informatics, 79*(11), 736–771.

Elkington, J. (1997). The triple bottom line. *Environmental Management: Readings and Cases, 2*, 49–66.

Eppmann, R., Bekk, M., & Klein, K. (2018). Gameful experience in gamification: Construction and validation of a gameful experience scale [GAMEX]. *Journal of Interactive Marketing, 43*(1), 98–115.

Eryılmaz, G., Unur, K., & Akgündüz, Y. (2021). How do flow experiences and emotional states of individuals participating in recreational activities affect their self-efficacy perceptions and life satisfaction? *Journal of Multidisciplinary Academic Tourism, 6*(2), 127–142.

Eseadi, C., & Ngwu, M. O. (2023). Significance of music therapy in treating depression and anxiety disorders among people with cancer. *World Journal of Clinical Oncology, 14*(2), 69.

Eswaran, H., Lal, R., & Reich, P. F. (2019). Land degradation: An overview. *Response to Land Degradation*, 20–35.

Faggini, M., Bruno, B., & Parziale, A. (2021). Creating value for a sustainable healthcare: The role of digital platforms. *Journal of Creating Value, 7*(2), 170–182.

Fama, E. F., & Jensen, M. C. (1983). Agency problems and residual claims. *The Journal of Law and Economics, 26*(2), 327–349.

Fanini, B., Pagano, A., Pietroni, E., Ferdani, D., Demetrescu, E., & Palombini, A. (2023). Augmented reality for cultural heritage. *Springer Handbook of Augmented Reality* (pp. 391–411). Springer International Publishing.

Fattahi, M., Farzin, M., Sadeghi, M., & Makvandi, R. (2022). Patient engagement behaviors in hospitals: The role of word of mouth and patient helping behaviors. *International Journal of Pharmaceutical and Healthcare Marketing, 16*(4), 606–623.

Fennell, D. A. (2021). Technology and the sustainable tourist in the new age of disruption. In *Routledge Handbook of Ecotourism* (pp. 83–90). Routledge.

Fenu, C., & Pittarello, F. (2018). Svevo tour: The design and the experimentation of an augmented reality application for engaging visitors of a literary museum. *International Journal of Human-Computer Studies, 114*, 20–35.

Fishbein, M., & Ajzen, I. (1977). *Belief, attitude, intention, and behavior: An introduction to theory and research.* Addison-Wesley.

Fisher, B., & Christopher, T. (2007). Poverty and biodiversity: Measuring the overlap of human poverty and the biodiversity hotspots. *Ecological Economics, 62*(1), 93–101.

Fitz-Walter, Z., Tjondronegoro, D., & Wyeth, P. (2011, November). Orientation passport: Using gamification to engage university students. In *Proceedings of the 23rd Australian computer-human interaction conference* (pp. 122–125).

Fornell, C., & Larcker, D. F. (1981). Evaluating structural equation models with unobservable variables and measurement error. *Journal of Marketing Research, 18*(1), 39–50.

Fürstenau, D., Gersch, M., & Schreiter, S. (2023). Digital therapeutics (DTx). *Business & Information Systems Engineering, 65*(3), 349–360.

Gajdzik, B., & Wolniak, R. (2022). Smart production workers in terms of creativity and innovation: The implication for open innovation. *Journal of Open Innovation: Technology, Market, and Complexity, 8*(2), 68.

Galetsi, P., Katsaliaki, K., & Kumar, S. (2023). Exploring benefits and ethical challenges in the rise of mHealth (mobile healthcare) technology for the common good: An analysis of mobile applications for health specialists. *Technovation, 121*, 102598.

Gao, H. (2022). Automatic recommendation of online music tracks based on deep learning. *Mathematical Problems in Engineering, 2022*(1), 5936156.

García, L., Parra, L., Jimenez, J. M., Lloret, J., & Lorenz, P. (2020). IoT-based smart irrigation systems: An overview on the recent trends on sensors and IoT systems for irrigation in precision agriculture. *Sensors, 20*(4), 1042.

Geissdoerfer, M., Bocken, N. M., & Hultink, E. J. (2016). Design thinking to enhance the sustainable business modelling process–A workshop based on a value mapping process. *Journal of Cleaner Production, 135*, 1218–1232.

Ghouaiel, N., Garbaya, S., Cieutat, J. M., & Jessel, J. P. (2017). Mobile augmented reality in museums: Towards enhancing visitor's learning experience. *International Journal of Virtual Reality, 17*(1), 21–31.

Giannattasio, A., Sestino, A., & Baima, G. (2024). Crafting a healthier future: exploring the nexus of product design, digital innovations and dynamic marketing for obesity prevention. A literature review. *British Food Journal, 126*(7), 2668–2685

Gill, P., Stewart, K., Treasure, E., & Chadwick, B. (2008). Methods of data collection in qualitative research: Interviews and focus groups. *British Dental Journal, 204*(6), 291–295.

Gjellebæk, C., Svensson, A., Bjørkquist, C., Fladeby, N., & Grundén, K. (2020). Management challenges for future digitalization of healthcare services. *Futures, 124*, 102636.

Gomiero, T., Pimentel, D., & Paoletti, M. G. (2011). Is there a need for a more sustainable agriculture? *Critical Reviews in Plant Sciences, 30*(1–2), 6–23.

Graziano, T., & Privitera, D. (2020). Cultural heritage, tourist attractiveness and augmented reality: Insights from Italy. *Journal of Heritage Tourism, 15*(6), 666–679.

Griskevicius, V., Tybur, J., & Van Den Bergh, B. (2010). Going Green to Be Seen: Status, Reputation, and Conspicious Conservation, *Journal of Personality and Social Psychology, 98*(3), 392–404.

Gu, D., Yang, X., Li, X., Jain, H. K., & Liang, C. (2018). Understanding the role of mobile internet-based health services on patient satisfaction and word-of-mouth. *International Journal of Environmental Research and Public Health, 15*(9), 1972.

Guido, G., Pichierri, M., Rizzo, C., Chieffi, V., & Moschis, G. (2020). Information processing by elderly consumers: A five-decade review. *Journal of Services Marketing, 35*(1), 14–28.

Gybel Jensen, C., Gybel Jensen, F., & Loft, M. I. (2024). Patients' Experiences With Digitalization in the Health Care System: Qualitative Interview Study. *Journal of Medical Internet Research, 26*, e47278.

Hackbarth, G., Grover, V., & Mun, Y. Y. (2003). Computer playfulness and anxiety: Positive and negative mediators of the system experience effect on perceived ease of use. *Information & Management, 40*(3), 221–232.

Hair, J. F., Black, W. C., Babin, B. J., Anderson, R. E., & Tatham, R. L. (2009). *Multivariate data analysis* (7th ed.). Pearson Prentice Hall.

Hair, J. F., Risher, J. J., Sarstedt, M., & Ringle, C. M. (2019). When to use and how to report the results of PLS-SEM. *European Business Review, 31*(1), 2–24.

Hamari, J., Koivisto, J., & Sarsa, H. (2014, January). Does gamification work?—A literature review of empirical studies on gamification. In *2014 47th Hawaii international conference on system sciences* (pp. 3025–3034). IEEE.

Han, D. I. D., Weber, J., Bastiaansen, M., Mitas, O., & Lub, X. (2019). Virtual and augmented reality technologies to enhance the visitor experience in cultural tourism. *Augmented reality and virtual reality: The power of AR and VR for business*, 113–128.

Hariri, N., Mobasher, B., & Burke, R. (2012, September). Context-aware music recommendation based on latenttopic sequential patterns. In *Proceedings of the sixth ACM conference on Recommender systems* (pp. 131–138).

Harris, L. C. (2002). Developing market orientation: An exploration of differences in management approaches. *Journal of Marketing Management, 18*(7–8), 603–632.

Hayes, A. F. (2018). Partial, conditional, and moderated moderated mediation: Quantification, inference, and interpretation. *Communication Monographs, 85*(1), 4–40.

Haynes, R. (2003). Geographical access to health care. *Access to Health Care*, 13–35.

Heinz, M., Martin, P., Margrett, J. A., Yearns, M., Franke, W., Yang, H. I., & Chang, C. K. (2013). Perceptions of technology among older adults. *Journal of Gerontological Nursing, 39*(1), 42–51.

Hemerling, J., Kilmann, J., Danoesastro, M., Stutts, L., & Ahern, C. (2018). It's not a digital transformation without a digital culture. *Boston Consulting Group*, 1–11.

Henseler, J., Ringle, C. M., & Sarstedt, M. (2015). A new criterion for assessing discriminant validity in variance-based structural equation modeling. *Journal of the Academy of Marketing Science, 43*, 115–135.

Hesmondhalgh, D., Campos Valverde, R., Kaye, D., & Li, Z. (2023). The impact of algorithmically driven recommendation systems on music consumption and production: A literature review. *UK Centre for Data Ethics and Innovation Reports*.

Himonides, E. (2022). Music, technology, and well-being. In *Applied Positive School Psychology* (pp. 134–141). Routledge.

Hoang, N. T., & Kanemoto, K. (2021). Mapping the deforestation footprint of nations reveals growing threat to tropical forests. *Nature Ecology & Evolution, 5*(6), 845–853.

Hoffman, D. L., Moreau, C. P., Stremersch, S., & Wedel, M. (2022). The rise of new technologies in marketing: A framework and outlook. *Journal of Marketing, 86*(1), 1–6.

Holdren, J. P. (2008). Science and technology for sustainable well-being. *Science, 319*(5862), 424–434.

Hollebeek, L. D., & Belk, R. (2021). Consumers' technology-facilitated brand engagement and wellbeing: Positivist TAM/PERMA-vs. Consumer Culture Theory perspectives. *International Journal of Research in Marketing, 38*(2), 387–401.

Hong, J. S., Wasden, C., & Han, D. H. (2021). Introduction of digital therapeutics. *Computer Methods and Programs in Biomedicine, 209*, 106319.

Hsee, C. K., & Hastie, R. (2006). Decision and experience: Why don't we choose what makes us happy? *Trends in Cognitive Sciences, 10*(1), 31–37.

Hsu, C. L., & Chen, M. C. (2018). How does gamification improve user experience? An empirical investigation on the antecedences and consequences of user experience and its mediating role. *Technological Forecasting and Social Change, 132*, 118–129.

Hu, X., Chen, J., & Wang, Y. (2021). University students' use of music for learning and well-being: A qualitative study and design implications. *Information Processing & Management, 58*(1), 102409.

Huang, W. H. Y., & Soman, D. (2013). Gamification of education. *Report Series: Behavioural Economics in Action, 29*(4), 37.

Hunter, P. (2019). Remote working in research: An increasing usage of flexible work arrangements can improve productivity and creativity. *EMBO Reports, 20*(1), e47435.

Huotari, K., & Hamari, J. (2012, October). Defining gamification: A service marketing perspective. In *Proceeding of the 16th international academic MindTrek conference* (pp. 17–22).

Ibáñez, M. B., Di Serio, Á., Villarán, D., & Kloos, C. D. (2014). Experimenting with electromagnetism using augmented reality: Impact on flow student experience and educational effectiveness. *Computers & Education, 71*, 1–13.

Inkster, B., Sarda, S., & Subramanian, V. (2018). An empathy-driven, conversational artificial intelligence agent (Wysa) for digital mental well-being: Real-world data evaluation mixed-methods study. *JMIR mHealth and uHealth, 6*(11), e12106.

International Federation of the Phonographic Industry. (2023). *Engaging with Music 2023: Global insights into music consumption.* Retrieved from https://www.ifpi.org/wp-content/uploads/2023/12/IFPI-Engaging-With-Music-2023_full-report.pdf

Jeong, H., Yoo, J. H., Goh, M., & Song, H. (2024). Deep breathing in your hands: Designing and assessing a DTx mobile app. *Frontiers in Digital Health, 6*, 1287340.

Jin, Y., Htun, N. N., Tintarev, N., & Verbert, K. (2019, June). Contextplay: Evaluating user control for context-aware music recommendation. In *Proceedings of the 27th ACM conference on user modeling, adaptation and personalization* (pp. 294–302).

Jones, C., Scholes, L., Johnson, D., Katsikitis, M., & Carras, M. C. (2014). Gaming well: Links between videogames and flourishing mental health. *Frontiers in Psychology, 5*, 76833.

Jung, S. R. (2006). *The perceived benefits of healthcare information technology adoption: Construct and survey development.* Louisiana State University and Agricultural & Mechanical College.

Jung, T., tom Dieck, M. C., Lee, H., & Chung, N. (2016, February 2–5). Effects of virtual reality and augmented reality on visitor experiences in museum. In *Information and communication technologies in tourism 2016: Proceedings of the international conference in Bilbao, Spain* (pp. 621–635). Springer International Publishing.

Juslin, P. N., & Västfjäll, D. (2008). Emotional responses to music: The need to consider underlying mechanisms. *Behavioral and Brain Sciences, 31*(5), 559–575.

Kahneman, D., & Krueger, A. B. (2006). Developments in the measurement of subjective well-being. *Journal of Economic Perspectives, 20*(1), 3–24.

Kang, H., & Lou, C. (2022). AI agency vs. human agency: Understanding human–AI interactions on TikTok and their implications for user engagement. *Journal of Computer-Mediated Communication, 27*(5), zmac014.

Karahanna, E., Straub, D. W., & Chervany, N. L. (1999). Information technology adoption across time: A cross-sectional comparison of pre-adoption and post-adoption beliefs. *MIS Quarterly*, 183–213.

Karahoca, A., Karahoca, D., & Aksöz, M. (2018). Examining intention to adopt to internet of things in healthcare technology products. *Kybernetes, 47*(4), 742–770.

Kari, T., Koivunen, S., Frank, L., Makkonen, M., & Moilanen, P. (2017). The expected and perceived wellbeing effects of short-term self-tracking technology use. *International Journal of Networking and Virtual Organisations, 17*(4), 354–370.

Katzner, T. E., & Arlettaz, R. (2020). Evaluating contributions of recent tracking-based animal movement ecology to conservation management. *Frontiers in Ecology and Evolution, 7*, 519.

Kaufman, N. (2019). Digital therapeutics: Leading the way to improved outcomes for people with diabetes. *Diabetes Spectrum, 32*(4), 301–303.

Kawasaki, S., Mills-Huffnagle, S., Aydinoglo, N., Maxin, H., & Nunes, E. (2022). Patient-and provider-reported experiences of a Mobile Novel Digital Therapeutic in People with Opioid Use Disorder (reSET-O): Feasibility and acceptability study. *JMIR Formative Research, 6*(3), e33073.

Kerr, J. T., & Ostrovsky, M. (2003). From space to species: Ecological applications for remote sensing. *Trends in Ecology & Evolution, 18*(6), 299–305.

Khan, N., Ray, R. L., Sargani, G. R., Ihtisham, M., Khayyam, M., & Ismail, S. (2021). Current progress and future prospects of agriculture technology: Gateway to sustainable agriculture. *Sustainability, 13*(9), 4883.

Kim, I., Azimi, E., Kazanzides, P., & Huang, C. M. (2023, October). Active Engagement with Virtual Reality Reduces Stress and Increases Positive Emotions. *In 2023 IEEE International Symposium on Mixed and Augmented Reality (ISMAR)* (pp. 523–532). IEEE.

Kim, S., Eom, J., & Shim, J. (2022). A Comparative Study on Intention to Use Digital Therapeutics: MZ Generation and Baby Boomers' Digital Therapeutics Use Intention in Korea. *International Journal of Environmental Research and Public Health, 19*(15), 9556.

Kitzinger, J. (1995). Qualitative Research: Introducing Focus Groups. *Bmj, 311*(7000), 299–302.

Kline, R. B. (2015). *Principles and practice of structural equation modeling* (4th ed.). The Guilford Press.

Koivisto, J., & Hamari, J. (2019). The rise of motivational information systems: A review of gamification research. *International Journal of Information Management, 45*, 191–210.

Koo, J. (2022). When I am Sad, I Don't Like AI: Preference for Music Playlists Curated by AI. *The Korean Journal of Consumer and Advertising Psychology, 23*(3), 207–226.

Koren, Y., Bell, R., & Volinsky, C. (2009). Matrix factorization techniques for recommender systems. *Computer, 42*(8), 30–37.

Kosaraju, R. (2021). How mobile devices are transforming healthcare. *Academia Letters, 18*, 1–14.

Kostrzewa, D., Chrobak, J., & Brzeski, R. (2024). Attributes relevance in content-based music recommendation system. *Applied Sciences, 14*(2), 855.

Kotler, P., & Armstrong, G. M. (2018). Marketing mix: Selected Chapters From: Principles of Marketing, Philip Kotler and Gary Armstrong. Pearson.

Kotler, P., Kartajaya, H., & Setiawan, I. (2022). *Marketing 5.0: Technology for humanity*. John Wiley & Sons.

Kraus, S., Jones, P., Kailer, N., Weinmann, A., Chaparro-Banegas, N., & Roig-Tierno, N. (2021). Digital transformation: An overview of the current state of the art of research. *SAGE Open, 11*(3), 21582440211047576.

Lambert, S. D., & Loiselle, C. G. (2008). Combining individual interviews and focus groups to enhance data richness. *Journal of Advanced Nursing, 62*(2), 228–237.

Lampropoulos, G., & Kinshuk. (2024). Virtual reality and gamification in education: A systematic review. *Educational Technology Research and Development*, 1–95.

Lapid, M. I., Atherton, P. J., Clark, M. M., Kung, S., Sloan, J. A., & Rummans, T. A. (2015). Cancer caregiver: Perceived benefits of technology. *Telemedicine and e-Health, 21*(11), 893–902.

Larsen, R. J., & Diener, E. (1985). A multitrait-multimethod examination of affect structure: Hedonic level and emotional intensity. *Personality and Individual Differences, 6*(5), 631–636.

Lehto, M. (2022). Cyber-attacks against critical infrastructure. *Cyber security: Critical infrastructure protection* (pp. 3–42). Springer International Publishing.

León, M. C., Nieto-Hipólito, J. I., Garibaldi-Beltrán, J., Amaya-Parra, G., Luque-Morales, P., Magaña-Espinoza, P., & Aguilar-Velazco, J. (2016). Designing a model of a digital ecosystem for healthcare and wellness using the business model canvas. *Journal of Medical Systems, 40*(6), 144.

Li, J., & Chang, X. (2021). Improving mobile health apps usage: A quantitative study on mPower data of Parkinson's disease. *Information Technology & People, 34*(1), 399–420.

Li, M., Ma, S., & Shi, Y. (2023). Examining the effectiveness of gamification as a tool promoting teaching and learning in educational settings: A meta-analysis. *Frontiers in Psychology, 14*, 1253549.

Lim, W. M., Jasim, K. M., & Das, M. (2024). Augmented and virtual reality in hotels: Impact on tourist satisfaction and intention to stay and return. *International Journal of Hospitality Management, 116*, 103631.

Lin, H. S., Ballhaus, W. F., & Chameau, J. L. (Ed.). (2014). Emerging and readily available technologies and national security: A framework for addressing ethical, legal, and societal issues. Summary.

Liu, Z. Y., Lomovtseva, N., & Korobeynikova, E. (2020). Online learning platforms: Reconstructing modern higher education. *International Journal of Emerging Technologies in Learning (iJET), 15*(13), 4–21.

Lv, Z. (2023). Generative artificial intelligence in the metaverse era. *Cognitive Robotics, 3*, 208–217.

Madadipouya, K., & Chelliah, S. (2017). A literature review on recommender systems algorithms, techniques and evaluations. *BRAIN. Broad Research in Artificial Intelligence and Neuroscience, 8*(2), 109–124.

Marasco, A., Buonincontri, P., Van Niekerk, M., Orlowski, M., & Okumus, F. (2018). Exploring the role of next-generation virtual technologies in destination marketing. *Journal of Destination Marketing & Management, 9*, 138–148.

Marchegiani, L., Nasta, L., & Pirolo, L. (2024). Adapting to the digital wave: Tour guides' role perception and technological integration in the cultural ecosystem. *European Journal of Cultural Management and Policy, 14*, 12846.

Maslowska, E., Malthouse, E. C., & Hollebeek, L. D. (2022). The role of recommender systems in fostering consumers' long-term platform engagement. *Journal of Service Management, 33*(4/5), 721–732.

Massi, M., D'Angelo, A. (2020). Reversing Heritage Destruction Through Digital Technology: The Rekrei Project. In Seychell, D., Dingli, A. (eds.), *Rediscovering Heritage Through Technology. Studies in Computational Intelligence* (vol. 859). Springer, Cham.

Matten, D., & Moon, J. (2008). "Implicit" and "explicit" CSR: A conceptual framework for a comparative understanding of corporate social responsibility. *Academy of Management Review, 33*(2), 404–424.

Mazzeo, M., & Zoccarato, F. (2020). What drives patients' acceptance of digital therapeutics? The interplay between rational and institutional factors.

McConnell, M. V., Turakhia, M. P., Harrington, R. A., King, A. C., & Ashley, E. A. (2018). Mobile health advances in physical activity, fitness, and atrial fibrillation: Moving hearts. *Journal of the American College of Cardiology, 71*(23), 2691–2701.

McDowell, I. (2010). Measures of self-perceived wellbeing. *Journal of Psychosomatic Research, 69*(1), 69–79.

McFee, B., Bertin-Mahieux, T., Ellis, D. P., & Lanckriet, G. R. (2012, April). The million-song dataset challenge. In *Proceedings of the 21st International Conference on World Wide Web* (pp. 909–916).

McLean, G., AlYahya, M., Barhorst, J. B., & Osei-Frimpong, K. (2023). Examining the influence of virtual reality tourism on consumers' subjective wellbeing. *Tourism Management Perspectives, 46*, 101088.

Menvielle, L., Audrain-Pontevia, A. F., & Menvielle, W. (Eds.). (2017). The digitization of healthcare: New challenges and opportunities.

Meredith, J. (1998). Building operations management theory through case and field research. *Journal of Operations Management, 16*(4), 441–454.

Merfeld, K., Wilhelms, M. P., & Henkel, S. (2019). Being driven autonomously–A qualitative study to elicit consumers' overarching motivational structures. *Transportation Research Part c: Emerging Technologies, 107*, 229–247.

Merriam, S. B., & Tisdell, E. J. (2015). *Qualitative Research: A Guide to Design and Implementation*. John Wiley & Sons.

Meyer, B., Utter, G. L., & Hillman, C. (2021). A personalized, interactive, cognitive behavioral therapy–based digital therapeutic (MODIA) for adjunctive treatment of opioid use disorder: Development study. *JMIR Mental Health, 8*(10), e31173.

Meythaler, A., Baumann, A., Krasnova, H., Hinz, O., & Spiekermann, S. (2023). Technology for Humanity. *Business & Information Systems Engineering, 65*(5), 487–496.

Mills, A. J., Durepos, G., & Wiebe, E. (Eds.). (2009). *Encyclopedia of Case Study Research*. Sage publications.

Montresor, S., & Vezzani, A. (2023). Digital technologies and eco-innovation. Evidence of the twin transition from Italian firms. *Industry and Innovation, 30*(7), 766–800.

Moulaei, K., Yadegari, A., Baharestani, M., Farzanbakhsh, S., Sabet, B., & Afrash, M. R. (2024). Generative artificial intelligence in healthcare: A scoping review on benefits, challenges and applications. *International Journal of Medical Informatics*, 105474.

Mowery, D. C. (2009). National security and national innovation systems. *The Journal of Technology Transfer, 34*(5), 455–473.

Naik, N., Hameed, B. Z., Sooriyaperakasam, N., Vinayahalingam, S., Patil, V., Smriti, K., & Somani, B. K. (2022). Transforming healthcare through a digital revolution: A review of digital healthcare technologies and solutions. *Frontiers in Digital Health, 4*, 919985.

Nandasena, W. D. K. V., Brabyn, L., & Serrao-Neumann, S. (2023). Using remote sensing for sustainable forest management in developing countries. *The palgrave handbook of global sustainability* (pp. 487–508). Springer International Publishing.

Nasta, L., & Pirolo, L. (2021). Digital Technologies to Fight the Pandemic Crisis: Evidence from the Vatican Museums. *International Journal of Business Research and Management (IJBRM), 12*(4), 163–174.

Navarro-Alamán, J., Lacuesta, R., García-Magariño, I., & Lloret, J. (2022). EmotIoT: An IoT system to improve users' wellbeing. *Applied Sciences, 12*(12), 5804.

Nawandar, N. K., & Satpute, V. R. (2019). IoT based low cost and intelligent module for smart irrigation system. *Computers and Electronics in Agriculture, 162*, 979–990.

Neumann, W., Martinuzzi, S., Estes, A. B., Pidgeon, A. M., Dettki, H., Ericsson, G., & Radeloff, V. C. (2015). Opportunities for the application of advanced remotely-sensed data in ecological studies of terrestrial animal movement. *Movement Ecology, 3*, 1–13.

Neves, C., Oliveira, T., & Karatzas, S. (2023). The impact of sustainable technologies in the perceived wellbeing: The role of intrinsic motivations. *International Journal of Human–Computer Interaction*, 1–12.

Nguyen, T. T., Grote, U., Neubacher, F., Do, M. H., & Paudel, G. P. (2023). Security risks from climate change and environmental degradation: Implications for sustainable land use transformation in the Global South. *Current Opinion in Environmental Sustainability, 63*, 101322.

Nofal, E., Panagiotidou, G., Reffat, R. M., Hameeuw, H., Boschloos, V., & Vande Moere, A. (2020). Situated tangible gamification of heritage for supporting collaborative learning of young museum visitors. *Journal on Computing and Cultural Heritage (JOCCH), 13*(1), 1–24.

Nwosu, A., Boardman, S., Husain, M. M., & Doraiswamy, P. M. (2022). Digital therapeutics for mental health: Is attrition the Achilles heel? *Frontiers in Psychiatry, 13*, 900615.

Obaideen, K., Yousef, B. A., AlMallahi, M. N., Tan, Y. C., Mahmoud, M., Jaber, H., & Ramadan, M. (2022). An overview of smart irrigation systems using IoT. *Energy Nexus, 7*, 100124.

Oderanti, F. O., Li, F., Cubric, M., & Shi, X. (2021). Business models for sustainable commercialisation of digital healthcare (eHealth) innovations for an increasingly ageing population. *Technological Forecasting and Social Change, 171*, 120969.

Oldenburg, J., Chase, D., Christensen, K. T., & Tritle, B. (Eds.). (2020). *Engage!: Transforming Healthcare Through Digital Patient Engagement*. CRC Press.

Ooi, K. B., Tan, G. W. H., Al-Emran, M., Al-Sharafi, M. A., Capatina, A., Chakraborty, A., & Wong, L. W. (2023). The potential of generative artificial intelligence across disciplines: Perspectives and future directions. *Journal of Computer Information Systems*, 1–32.

Orsolini, L., Longo, G., & Volpe, U. (2024). Practical application of digital therapeutics in people with mood disorders. *Current Opinion in Psychiatry, 37*(1), 9–17.

Ortega-Gras, J. J., Bueno-Delgado, M. V., Cañavate-Cruzado, G., & Garrido-Lova, J. (2021). Twin transition through the implementation of industry 4.0 technologies: Desk-research analysis and practical use cases in Europe. *Sustainability, 13*(24), 13601.

Osipov, V. S., & Skryl, T. V. (2021). Impact of digital technologies on the efficiency of healthcare delivery. In *IoT in Healthcare and Ambient Assisted Living* (pp. 243–261). Springer Singapore.

Osterwalder, A., & ve Pigneur, Y. (2010). Business Model Generation: A Handbook for Visionaries, Game Changers, and Challengers.

Ozdemir, M., Sahin, C., Arcagok, S., & Demır, M. K. (2018). The effect of augmented reality applications in the learning process: A meta-analysis study. *Eurasian Journal of Educational Research, 18*(74), 165–186.

Paiva, S., Ahad, M. A., Tripathi, G., Feroz, N., & Casalino, G. (2021). Enabling technologies for urban smart mobility: Recent trends, opportunities and challenges. *Sensors, 21*(6), 2143.

Palmatier, R. W., & Crecelius, A. T. (2019). The "first principles" of marketing strategy. *Ams Review, 9*, 5–26.

Palmer, J. (2002). *Environmental education in the 21st century: Theory, practice, progress and promise*. Routledge.

Parente, C. A., Salvatore, D., Gallo, G. M., & Cipollini, F. (2018). Using overbooking to manage no-shows in an Italian healthcare center. *BMC Health Services Research, 18*, 1–12.

Peters, A., & Dütschke, E. (2014). How do consumers perceive electric vehicles? A comparison of German consumer groups. *Journal of Environmental Policy & Planning, 16*(3), 359–377.

Phan, P., Mitragotri, S., & Zhao, Z. (2023). Digital therapeutics in the clinic. *Bioengineering & Translational Medicine, 8*(4), e10536.

Picard, R. W. (2000). *Affective computing.* MIT press.

Plekhanov, D., Franke, H., & Netland, T. H. (2022). Digital transformation: A review and research agenda. *European Management Journal, 41*(6), 821–844.

Podsakoff, P. M., MacKenzie, S. B., Lee, J. Y., & Podsakoff, N. P. (2003). Common method biases in behavioral research: A critical review of the literature and recommended remedies. *Journal of Applied Psychology, 88*(5), 879.

Porter, M. E., & Heppelmann, J. E. (2014). How smart, connected products are transforming competition. *Harvard Business Review, 92*(11), 64–88.

Pronk, N., Kleinman, D. V., Goekler, S. F., Ochiai, E., Blakey, C., & Brewer, K. H. (2021). Promoting health and well-being in healthy people 2030. *Journal of Public Health Management and Practice, 27*(Supplement 6), S242–S248.

Rauschnabel, P. A., Felix, R., & Hinsch, C. (2019). Augmented reality marketing: How mobile AR-apps can improve brands through inspiration. *Journal of Retailing and Consumer Services, 49*, 43–53.

Recchia, G., Capuano, D. M., Mistri, N., & Verna, R. (2020). Digital therapeutics-what they are, what they will be. *Acta Scientific Medical Sciences, 4*(3), 1–9.

Reker, G. T., & Wong, P. T. (1984). Psychological and physical wellbeing in the elderly: The Perceived Wellbeing Scale (PWB). *Canadian Journal on Aging/la Revue Canadienne Du Vieillissement, 3*(1), 23–32.

Rhoades, L., & Eisenberger, R. (2002). Perceived organizational support: A review of the literature. *Journal of Applied Psychology, 87*(4), 698.

Rizzo, C., Sestino, A., Gutuleac, R., & Bertoldi, B. (2023). Managing food-wasting: The role of customer cooperation in influencing firms' pro-environmental behavior. *Management Decision.*

Robeyns, I. (2020). Wellbeing, place and technology. *Wellbeing, Space and Society, 1*, 100013.

Rogozinski, B., Greenleaf, W., Sackman, J., & Cahana, A. (2018). Digital therapeutics in the management of chronic pain. *Handbook of Pain and Palliative Care: Biopsychosocial and Environmental Approaches for the Life Course*, 601–621.

Rossetti, G., Jepson, A., & Albanese, V. E. (2024). Food festivals and well-being: Extending the PERMA model. *Annals of Tourism Research, 107*, 10377.

Rozenblum, R., & Bates, D. W. (2013). Patient-centred healthcare, social media and the internet: The perfect storm? *BMJ Quality & Safety, 22*(3), 183–186.

Rudel, T. (2023). Population, development and tropical deforestation: a cross-national study. In *The Causes of Tropical Deforestation* (pp. 96–105). Routledge.

Sabherwal, R., & Grover, V. (2024). The societal impacts of generative artificial intelligence: A balanced perspective. *Journal of the Association for Information Systems, 25*(1), 13–22.

Sahoo, S., Sahoo, J., Kumar, S., Lim, W. M., & Ameen, N. (2023). Distance is no longer a barrier to healthcare services: Current state and future trends of telehealth research. *Internet Research, 33*(3), 890–944.

Sailer, M., Hense, J. U., Mayr, S. K., & Mandl, H. (2017). How gamification motivates: An experimental study of the effects of specific game design elements on psychological need satisfaction. *Computers in Human Behavior, 69*, 371–380.

Sangeetha, B. P., Kumar, N., Ambalgi, A. P., Haleem, S. L. A., Thilagam, K., & Vijayakumar, P. (2022). IOT based smart irrigation management system for environmental sustainability in India. *Sustainable Energy Technologies and Assessments, 52*, 101973.

Sarafim-Silva, B. A. M., Valente, V. B., Duarte, G. D., Nishida, C. K. S., Fani, E. F. G., Miyahara, G. I., & Bernabé, D. G. (2019). Emotional factors are critical motivators for tobacco use according to smokers' own perception. *Journal of Public Health, 27*, 499–506.

Schaltegger, S., & Burritt, R. (2018). Business cases and corporate engagement with sustainability: Differentiating ethical motivations. *Journal of Business Ethics, 147*, 241–259.

Schedl, M., Knees, P., & Gouyon, F. (2017, August). New paths in music recommender systems research. In *Proceedings of the Eleventh ACM Conference on Recommender Systems* (pp. 392–393).

Schedl, M., Zamani, H., Chen, C. W., Deldjoo, Y., & Elahi, M. (2018). Current challenges and visions in music recommender systems research. *International Journal of Multimedia Information Retrieval, 7*, 95.

Schiavone, F., Mancini, D., Leone, D., & Lavorato, D. (2021). Digital Business Models and ridesharing for value co-creation in healthcare: A multi-stakeholder ecosystem analysis. *Technological Forecasting and Social Change, 166*, 120647.

Schwarzer, R., & Luszczynska, A. (2008). Self efficacy. *Handbook of Positive Psychology Assessment, 2*, 7–217.

Seaborn, K., & Fels, D. I. (2015). Gamification in theory and action: A survey. *International Journal of Human-Computer Studies, 74*, 14–31.

Seawright, J., & Gerring, J. (2008). Case selection techniques in case study research: A menu of qualitative and quantitative options. *Political Research Quarterly, 61*(2), 294–308.

Seligman, M. E. P. (2011). Flourish: A Visionary New Understanding of Happiness and Well-Being. Free Press.

Senbekov, M., Saliev, T., Bukeyeva, Z., Almabayeva, A., Zhanaliyeva, M., Aitenova, N., & Fakhradiyev, I. (2020). The recent progress and applications of digital technologies in healthcare: A review. *International Journal of Telemedicine and Applications, 2020*(1), 8830200.

Sestino, A., Giraldi, L., Cedrola, E., Zamani, S. Z., & Guido, G. (2022). The business opportunity of blockchain value creation among the Internet of value. *Global Business Review*, 09721509221115012.

Sestino, A., Bernardo, A., Rizzo, C., & Bresciani, S. (2023). An explorative analysis of the antecedents and consequents of gamification in the digital therapeutic context. *European Journal of Innovation Management*.

Sestino, A., Kahlawi, A., & De Mauro, A. (2023). Decoding the data economy: A literature review of its impact on business, society and digital transformation. *European Journal of Innovation Management*.

Sestino, A. & Sagona, A. (2024). Enhancing Green and Sustainable Consumption Trough The Use of Blockchain-based Digital Technologies: The Roles and Corporate Social Responsibility, and Consumer Environmental Self-Efficacy. Evidences from Sustainable Olive Oil and Wine Production. Accepted, in the *3rd Engage EU Conference, Responsible Production and Consumption: Current Issues and Advances towards SDG12*, Nov. 21–22, 2024, University of National and World Economy, Sofia, Bulgaria.

Sestino, A., & D'Angelo, A. (2024). Elderly patients' reactions to gamification-based digital therapeutics (DTx): The relevance of socialization tendency seeking. *Technological Forecasting and Social Change, 205*, 123526.

Sestino, A., Prete, M. I., Piper, L., & Guido, G. (2020a). Internet of Things and Big Data as enablers for business digitalization strategies. *Technovation, 98*, 102173.

Sestino, A., Peluso, A. M., Amatulli, C., & Guido, G. (2022b). Let me drive you! The effect of change seeking and behavioral control in the Artificial Intelligence-based self-driving cars. *Technology in Society, 70*, 102017.

Shilpa, & Kaur, T. (2022). Digital healthcare: Current trends, challenges and future perspectives. In *Proceedings of the Future Technologies Conference (FTC) 2021, Volume 2* (pp. 645–661). Springer International Publishing.

Shin, H. R., Kim, S. K., & Kim, Y. S. (2020). Effect of self-efficacy of middle-aged and elderly on the intention to use digital health devices: Focusing on the difference between middle-aged and elderly. *Journal of Digital Convergence, 18*(10), 13–22.

Silvester, S., & Kurian, S. (2023, December). Recommendation Systems: Enhancing Personalization and Customer Experience. In *2023 3rd International Conference on Smart Generation Computing, Communication and Networking* (pp. 1–6). IEEE.

Silvestre, B. S., & Ţîrcă, D. M. (2019). Innovations for sustainable development: Moving toward a sustainable future. *Journal of Cleaner Production, 208,* 325–332.

Stankov, U., & Gretzel, U. (2020). Tourism 4.0 technologies and tourist experiences: A human-centered design perspective. *Information Technology & Tourism, 22*(3), 477–488.

Stewart, F., & James, J. (2019). *The economics of new technology in developing countries.* Routledge.

Strømmen-Bakhtiar, A. (2020). Introduction to Digital Transformation: and its impact on society. *Informing Science Press.*

Sundar, S. S. (2020). Rise of machine agency: A framework for studying the psychology of human–AI interaction (HAII). *Journal of Computer-Mediated Communication, 25*(1), 74–88.

Suryadi, Y., FoEh, J. E., & Manafe, H. (2022). Employee Productivity Determination: In Work Life Balance (WLB), Work From Home (WFH), Information Technology (IT) and Work Flexibility. *Indonesian Interdisciplinary Journal of Sharia Economics (IIJSE), 5*(2), 730–750.

Tanniru, M. (2019). Engagement leading to empowerment—Digital innovation strategies for patient care continuity. *Journal of Hospital Management and Health Policy, 3.*

Tarrant, M., North, A. C., & Hargreaves, D. J. (2000). English and American adolescents' reasons for listening to music. *Psychology of Music, 28*(2), 166–173.

Taylor, R., Davis, C., Brandt, J., Parker, M., Stäuble, T., & Said, Z. (2020). The rise of big data and supporting technologies in keeping watch on the world's forests. *International Forestry Review, 22*(1), 129–141.

Tom Dieck, M. C., & Jung, T. H. (2017). Value of augmented reality at cultural heritage sites: A stakeholder approach. *Journal of Destination Marketing & Management, 6*(2), 110–117.

Tranfield, D., Denyer, D., & Smart, P. (2003). Towards a methodology for developing evidence-informed management knowledge by means of systematic review. *British Journal of Management, 14*(3), 207–222.

Tussyadiah, I. P., Jung, T. H., & Tom Dieck, M. C. (2018). Embodiment of wearable augmented reality technology in tourism experiences. *Journal of Travel Research, 57*(5), 597–611.

van der Zant, T., Kouw, M., & Schomaker, L. (2013). *Generative artificial intelligence* (pp. 107–120). Springer.

van Kessel, R., Roman-Urrestarazu, A., Anderson, M., Kyriopoulos, I., Field, S., Monti, G., & Mossialos, E. (2023). Mapping factors that affect the uptake of digital therapeutics within health systems: Scoping review. *Journal of Medical Internet Research, 25,* e48000.

Van Veldhoven, Z., & Vanthienen, J. (2022). Digital transformation as an interaction-driven perspective between business, society, and technology. *Electronic Markets, 32*(2), 629–644.

Velankar, M., & Kulkarni, P. (2022). Music recommendation systems: overview and challenges. *Advances in Speech and Music Technology: Computational Aspects and Applications,* 51–69.

Velez, F. F., Colman, S., Kauffman, L., Ruetsch, C., & Anastassopoulos, K. (2021). Real-world reduction in healthcare resource utilization following treatment of opioid use disorder with reSET-O, a novel prescription digital therapeutic. *Expert Review of Pharmacoeconomics & Outcomes Research, 21*(1), 69–76.

Venkatesh, V., Thong, J. Y., & Xu, X. (2012). Consumer acceptance and use of information technology: Extending the unified theory of acceptance and use of technology. *MIS Quarterly, 36*(1), 157–178.

Venkatesh, V., & Bala, H. (2008). Technology acceptance model 3 and a research agenda on interventions. *Decision Sciences, 39*(2), 273–315.

Venkatesh, V., & Davis, F. D. (1996). A model of the antecedents of perceived ease of use: Development and test. *Decision Sciences, 27*(3), 451–481.

Venkatesh, V., & Davis, F. D. (2000). A theoretical extension of the technology acceptance model: Four longitudinal field studies. *Management Science, 46*(2), 186–204.

Vohs, K. D., & Baumeister, R. F. (Eds.). (2016). *Handbook of self-regulation: Research, theory, and applications.* Guilford Publications.

Waegemann, C. P. (2010). MHealth: The next generation of telemedicine? *Telemedicine and e-Health, 16*(1), 23–26.

Wan, C. K. B., & Onuike, A. J. (2021). Illuminating opportunities for smart tourism innovation that foster sustainable tourist well-being using Q methodology. *Sustainability, 13*(14), 7929.

Wang, F., Harindintwali, J. D., Yuan, Z., Wang, M., Wang, F., Li, S., & Chen, J. M. (2021). Technologies and perspectives for achieving carbon neutrality. *The Innovation, 2*(4), 100180.

Wang, C. Y., Wang, Y. C., & Chou, S. C. T. (2018). A context and emotion aware system for personalized music recommendation. *Journal of Internet Technology, 19*(3), 765–779.

Wang, D., Zhang, X., Yin, Y., Yu, D., Xu, G., & Deng, S. (2023). Multi-view enhanced graph attention network for session-based music recommendation. *ACM Transactions on Information Systems, 42*(1), 1–30.

Wang, H., Zhou, W., Li, Y., & Li, Y. (2024). Business process digitisation and firm innovation performance: The role of knowledge search and digital culture. *Knowledge Management Research & Practice, 22*(1), 49–60.

Warner, K., Hamza, M., Oliver-Smith, A., Renaud, F., & Julca, A. (2010). Climate change, environmental degradation and migration. *Natural Hazards, 55*, 689–715.

Webster, F. E., Jr. (2005). A perspective on the evolution of marketing management. *Journal of Public Policy & Marketing, 24*(1), 121–126.

Weng, C., Tran, K. N. P., Yang, C. C., Huang, H. I., & Chen, H. (2024). Can an augmented reality-integrated gamification approach enhance vocational high school students' learning outcomes and motivation in an electronics course? *Education and Information Technologies, 29*(4), 4025–4053.

Wherton, J., Greenhalgh, T., Hughes, G., & Shaw, S. E. (2022). The role of information infrastructures in scaling up video consultations during COVID-19: Mixed methods case study into opportunity, disruption, and exposure. *Journal of Medical Internet Research, 24*(11), e42431.

Wich, S. A., Hudson, M., Andrianandrasana, H., & Longmore, S. N. (2021). Drones for conservation. *Conservation Technology, 35*.

Wolf, G. (2017). New challenges of the digital transformation: the comeback of the vision-mission system. *Out-thinking Organizational Communications: The Impact of Digital Transformation*, 113–128.

Wu, X., Tian, Z., & Guo, J. (2022). A review of the theoretical research and practical progress of carbon neutrality. *Sustainable Operations and Computers, 3*, 54–66.

Xi, N., & Hamari, J. (2019). Does gamification satisfy needs? A study on the relationship between gamification features and intrinsic need satisfaction. *International Journal of Information Management, 46*, 210–221.

Xu, W., Dainoff, M. J., Ge, L., & Gao, Z. (2023). Transitioning to human interaction with AI systems: New challenges and opportunities for HCI professionals to enable human-centered AI. *International Journal of Human-Computer Interaction, 39*(3), 494–518.

Yang, S., Gao, B., Jiang, L., Jin, J., Gao, Z., Ma, X., & Woo, W. L. (2018). IoT structured long-term wearable social sensing for mental wellbeing. *IEEE Internet of Things Journal, 6*(2), 3652–3662.

Yin, R. K. (2013). Validity and generalization in future case study evaluations. *Evaluation, 19*(3), 321–332.

Yin, R. K. (2018). *Case study research and applications* (Vol. 6). Sage.

Zaoui, F., & Souissi, N. (2020). Roadmap for digital transformation: A literature review. *Procedia Computer Science, 175*, 621–628.

Zook, C., & Allen, J. (2001). Profit from the core: Growth strategy in an era of turbulence. *Harvard Business School Press*.

Zott, C., & Amit, R. (2010). Business model design: An activity system perspective. *Long Range Planning, 43*(2–3), 216–226.

The manufacturer's authorised representative in the EU is Springer
Nature Customer Service Centre GmbH, Europaplatz 3, 69115 Heidelberg,
Germany. If you have any concerns regarding our products, please
contact ProductSafety@springernature.com

Printed and bound by CPI Group (UK) Ltd, Croydon, CR0 4YY
27/04/2026
02097604-0001